Music in Puerto Rico

A Reader's Anthology

Edited and translated by

Donald Thompson

The Scarecrow Press, Inc.
Lanham, Maryland, and London
2002

SCARECROW PRESS, INC.

Published in the United States of America
by Scarecrow Press, Inc.
4720 Boston Way, Lanham, Maryland 20706
www.scarecrowpress.com

4 Pleydell Gardens, Folkestone
Kent CT20 2DN, England

British Library Cataloguing in Publication Information Available

Library of Congress Cataloging-in-Publication Data Available

ISBN 0-8108-3914-8

♾™ The paper used in this publication meets the minimum requirements of
American National Standard for Information Sciences—Permanence of
Paper for Printed Library Materials, ANSI/NISO Z39.48-1992.
Manufactured in the United States of America.

CONTENTS

Urban Popular and Commercial Music

PREFACE

The recorded history of the Caribbean island of Puerto Rico begins at the end of the fifteenth century, when Christopher Columbus came upon the island of Borikén during his second voyage to what would become known as the New World. Accompanying the Columbus expedition was Fray Ramón Pané, a self-characterized humble friar whose report of the beliefs and customs of the aboriginal inhabitants of the neighboring island of Hispaniola (today's Haiti and the Dominican Republic) is conventionally taken as valid for Borikén (today's Puerto Rico) as well. That premise accepted, Fray Ramón's writings were the first of a long line of comments, descriptions, and studies of Puerto Rican life, including the lively arts of music and dance. The earliest reports, as well as writings extending into the nineteenth century, tended to describe only those aspects which were found exotic, strange, or reprehensible by European commentators. Only in the nineteenth century did native writers, as well as transplanted peninsular Spaniards and other observers, turn their attention directly toward matters of social life, but again often focusing on what the city-bred writers found exotic or primitive in the customs and behavior of rural islanders.

A new element was introduced early in the nineteenth century by the many traveling lyric theater companies and individual performers who visited the island on their way to South America from Europe and the United States. The reviewing of concerts, operas, and zarzuelas began in the Puerto Rican press, while debates over the propriety of the native *danza* became both contentious and widespread.

The twentieth century brought many changes to Puerto Rico, not the least of which were traumatic shifts caused by the change of political sovereignty, from Spain to the United States, that occurred in 1898 at the end of the Spanish-American War. A period of deep economic depression, lasting for decades, was accompanied by a realignment of political forces and cultural energies. Further changes occurred in the 1950s, when the insular government, riding an unprecedented wave of eco-

nomic progress and industrial development, first became heavily involved in the arts, in realms of policy and production as well as in sharp-
ly focused large-scale support and promotion. The Puerto Rico Casals
Festival, conceived in 1956 and launched the following year, represented
an early and pivotal flowering of this singular governmental initiative.
Vastly improved means of transportation and communication with the
broader world have further transformed Puerto Rican life during subsequent decades, and it is essentially a new Puerto Rico which faces the
twenty-first century.

Five centuries of musical life in Puerto Rico have been recorded by
writers beginning with the observations of early Spanish chroniclers and,
especially during the past century and a half, in an expanding literature
embracing the work of romanticizing regionalists, visiting folklorists,
newspaper and magazine writers, researchers and scholars, and more recently, the authors of masters' theses and doctoral dissertations. Some of
this writing, especially during recent decades, has been conceived and
published in English. However, the great bulk of significant writing
about music in Puerto Rico exists only in Spanish, with a small quantity
in French and other languages.

Those in search of original sources can find the nineteenth century
Puerto Rican newspapers and magazines quoted here in the Puerto Rican
Collection of the University of Puerto Rico General Library (Río Piedras); the same library's Josefina del Toro Rare Books Collection
possesses a number of first editions of the early Spanish chroniclers and
historians. More recent books cited here can be seen in many university
libraries with extensive Latin American collections.

Little of the early writing is easily accessible through the more accustomed routes of bibliographic search. It thus escapes the notice of
many of those who might profit most by its study: anglophone scholars,
teachers, students, members of the Puerto Rican diaspora, and others
interested in this vital aspect of Puerto Rican life. The present anthology,
representing a small fraction of what has been written about music in
Puerto Rico, is offered in that spirit.

1

CHRONICLERS OF CONQUEST: ABORIGINAL MUSIC OBSERVED AND ENVISIONED

Direct knowledge of the music and dance of the aboriginal inhabitants of the island of Puerto Rico is nonexistent, for reports based on direct observation at the time of the Spanish conquest are lacking and the indigenous population was effectively obliterated within a few years. However, it is believed, on the basis of early reports supported by archeological evidence, that the aboriginal Puerto Ricans were of the same Taíno race as their neighbors on the other islands of the Greater Antilles: Hispaniola, Cuba, and Jamaica. Early descriptions of music, dance and ritual on those islands are not plentiful but they do exist, providing a basis for surmise regarding Puerto Rico. These accounts must be treated with caution, for most descriptions have simply repeated and elaborated material composed by earlier writers in an unquestioning chain going back to the first chroniclers themselves. In addition, the early chroniclers and historians viewed their subject through their own conceptual lenses and relying upon descriptive language which could only draw upon comparisons with what they had seen or heard of in Europe. Too, writers tended to freely mix reports from the Antilles with information originating in Central America and the South American mainland.

And finally, the earliest writers—Pané, Las Casas, Oviedo—had particular interests to advance. Although this would not necessarily affect their description of musical instruments and other sound-producers, depictions already affected by the factors just mentioned, it could very definitely affect their accounts of rituals and other communal activities, particularly those perceived as religious in nature. The sixteenth century, we must remember, was not an age of scientific reporting.[1]

1

A Taíno Musical Instrument

Fr. Ramón Pané, "Relación de las antigüedades de los indios," in Fernando Colón, *Historie del S.D. Fernando Colombo: Nelle quali s'ha particolare, & vera relatione della vita, & de'fatti dell'Ammiraglio D. Christoforo Colombo sua padre,* transl. from Spanish by Alfonso Ulloa (Venice: Francesco de Franceschi, 1571), fols. 126 verso; 127 recto; 133 verso.[2]

By order of the illustrious Admiral, Viceroy, and Governor of the Islands and Lands of the Indies, I, Fray Ramón, a poor brother of the Order of St. Jerome, describe what I have been able to discover and learn of the beliefs and idolatries of the Indians, and of how they worship their gods.

XIV. Of Whence Come These Beliefs and Why the Indians Preserve Them

Practicing among them are men called *bohutis*, who perpetrate many deceits and falsehoods as we shall later explain, to make the Indians believe that they speak with the dead and that they know all of the Indians' actions and secrets, and that when the Indians fall ill the *bohutis* cure them, deceiving them in this way. I have seen part of this with my own eyes, although of other things I have only repeated what I have heard from many Indians, especially from the leaders, with whom I have spoken more than with others, because the leaders are firmer in their beliefs than the other Indians. As do the Moors, the Indians preserve their laws in ancient songs by which they are ruled, as the Moors are ruled by their scriptures. When they wish to sing these songs they play a certain instrument called *mayohavau*, which is hollow and made of strong and very thin wood, an arm's length long and half as wide. The part which is played upon is made in the form of a blacksmith's tongs and the other end looks like a club, so that the instrument resembles a gourd with a long neck. This instrument is so sonorous that it can be heard a league and a half away. To it the Indians sing their songs, which they learn by memory. The instrument is played by the leaders, who learn to play it as children and sing to its accompaniment as is their custom.

An Early Chronicler

Fray Bartolomé de las Casas, *Apologética historia de las Indias*. Vol. 1, *Historiadores de Indias*, Manuel Serrano y Sanz, ed. (Madrid: Bailley, Balliere e Hijos, 1909.Vol. 13, *Nueva biblioteca de autores españoles*, Marcelino Menéndez y Pelayo, ed.), Chap. 104, 537-38.[3]

[The aborigines] were very fond of their dances, performed to the sound of the songs which they chanted and of hoarse wooden drums constructed without skins or anything else added. Their rhythm was fascinating to observe both in the voices and in the dance steps, for some three or four hundred men would unite with the arms of each placed on the shoulders of his neighbor. Neither foot of any dancer extended farther than the other one, and all the dancers were perfectly aligned. For their part, the women danced with the same rhythm, the same music, and the same order. The words of their songs referred to ancient matters and sometimes to childish things, such as "Tal pescadillo se tomó desta manera y se huyó" or similar expressions as I understood them at the time. Whenever groups of women came together to grate the cassava root from which they made bread, they would sing a very attractive song.

The Areíto

Gonzalo Fernández de Oviedo y Valdés, *Historia general y natural de las Indias, islas y tierra-firme del mar océano* (Seville: Juan Cromberger, 1525), fol. xlv verso.[4]

Book V. Chapter 1, which treats of the diabolical images which the Indians possess and of their idolatries, and of the areítos and dances that they perform while singing, and of the manner in which they retain in their memory past occurrences which they wish to preserve for their descendants and for the community.

Let us now consider their *areítos* or chants, the second thing which I promised in the title of this chapter. These people had a different way of remembering ancient things from the past. This was by way of their chants and dances, which they called *areítos*, the same thing that we would describe as dancing while singing. Livy says that the first dancers came to Rome from Etruria and organized their songs so that the voices would conform to the dancers' movements. . . . I believe that this must have been similar to the *areítos* or communal singing of these Indians.

The *areíto* was performed as follows. For the pleasure of commemorating some great event, or simply as a pastime, many Indians would gather together, sometimes only the men or only the women; men and women would become intermixed during general celebration, or to mark a victory or the defeat of enemies, or for the wedding of a chief or the king of the region and on other occasions of general enjoyment. To increase their pleasure or rejoicing they sometimes grasped hands or linked arms; sometimes they moved in single file (or in a circle) as one of them (either a man or woman) served as the leader. The leader would execute certain steps forward and backward in a very ordered fashion, to be immediately repeated by the group. The *areíto* would progress in this alternating fashion, as the group would repeat the phrases sung by the leader in a loud or soft voice, doing whatever the leader said and did, with the steps all very measured and adapted to the verses or words which were sung. And as the leader indicated, the group would respond with the same words, the same steps, the same patterns; during the group's response the leader would be silent, while still maintaining the steps of the dance. After each response, each repetition of the leader's words, the leader would immediately continue with another verse or other words, which the group would repeat. In this uninterrupted fashion the event would last three or four hours or more, until the leader's tale was completed; at times an *areíto* could extend from one day to the next. Sometimes, together with the singing, a drum would be used, made from a hollowed log, more or less the size of a man according to their wishes and sounding like the muffled drums of the blacks. Instead of using a head of skin they pierce the wood with a series of holes and perforations through which the instrument sounds in an unpleasant fashion. And in this way, with or without that disagreeable instrument, they recite their memories and their past history as we have described, recounting in these songs how their chiefs died, and who and how many they were, and other things which they do not wish to forget. Sometimes they change leaders, and continue the same account with new music and new steps or begin another, if the previous one has finished, with the same music or a new chant.

This kind of dancing seems similar to the songs and dances of the workers, when in certain parts of Spain in the summertime men and women entertain themselves with kites and tambourines; in Flanders I have seen the same kind of singing as men and women dance in groups responding to a person who leads them or anticipates their singing, as has been noted. During the time when Fray Nicolás Ovando governed this island as supreme commandant, an *areíto* took place before Anacaona, the wife of chief or king Caonabo and a great lady; more than 300 young ladies took part, all servants of Anacaona and all virgins, because she did not want married women or women who had known men to participate in the *areíto*.

Returning to our theme, this type of singing, which is known on this island and others as well as in a great part of *tierra firme*, is a recounting of the history of past occurrences such as wars as well as events during periods of peace, because by the repetition of such songs the deeds and the events are not forgotten. Instead of books it is these songs which remain in the memory; in this way they recite the genealogies of their chiefs or kings or lords, and their works, and the good or bad seasons which they have experienced or are experiencing, and other things which they wish to communicate to young and old alike, or which they wish to be widely known and firmly engraved in the memory. And for this purpose the *areítos* continue, so that they not be forgotten, especially the accounts of famous victories during battle.

During this singing and dancing other Indians serve refreshment to the dancers, who do not stop dancing as they drink but continue moving their feet as they drink what is given them. And these refreshments are certain beverages used by these Indians. When the ceremony is over most of them, men and women alike, remain for a long time drunk and senseless on the ground. When a dancer becomes drunk during the ceremony he is removed from the group and the dancing continues; the *areíto* thus ends in general drunkenness. This occurs in cases of solemn *areítos* performed during weddings or burials, or in connection with battles, or to celebrate some victory; other kinds of *areíto* are often performed without ending in drunkenness. In this manner everyone knows this way of recounting history, some having learned it only for the carousing and others to learn this kind of music. Sometimes similar songs and dances are newly created by persons who are noted among the Indians for their ingenuity and for their gift of inventiveness.

□   □   □

Pietro Martire d'Anghiera (Petrus Martyr; Peter Martyr; Pedro Mártir de Anglería), *Décadas del Nuevo Mundo*, 2 vols., transl. from Latin by Agustín Millares Carlo, Edmundo O'Gorman, ed. (México: José Porrúa e Hijos, Sucesores, 1964-65. Vol. 6, *Biblioteca José Porrúa Estrada de historia mexicana,* Jorge Gurria Lacroix, ed. *Primera serie: La Conquista*). (A) 1, 195 (Decade 1, Book 9); (B) 1, 351-52 (Decade 3, Book 6); (C) 2, 643-44 (Decade 7, Book 10).[5]

(A) Asked about the origin of such useless rituals, which are like a plague, [natives of Hispaniola] answered that they had received them from their ancestors, and that from time immemorial certain verses are preserved which are not to be taught to anyone except the sons of chieftans. These verses are committed to memory, for the natives are illiterate, and are sung before the community as solemn rites. The natives have only one musical instrument, made of wood, hollow and resonant, which they strike like a drum.

Teaching them these superstitions are their wizards, who are also physicians who perpetrate a thousand deceptions on the ignorant populace, obliging them by their great authority to believe that they speak with the *zemes*[6] themselves and that they can predict the future. And if some invalid should recover, the wizards convince him that it has been due to the benevolence of the *zeme.*

(B) From time immemorial, and particularly in the residences of the kings, it is customary that the *boicos* or sages teach the noble sons in the knowledge of things, by memory. Through this teaching two ends are sought: one is general, dealing with the origin and sequence of historical events; the other deals with the memorable deeds in peace and war of the boys' fathers, grandfathers, great grandfathers and other ancestors. Both teachings are preserved in verses called *areítos,* and as occurs with our *cítara* players, they sing their verses, accompanying them with dancing to the sound of drums built according to their custom and called *maguey.* They also have amorous, sad and warlike *areítos,* their melodies perfectly adapted to their purpose. They also have dances, in which they display much more agility than is seen in our dances, for they are not worried about anything else and as they dance nude they can dance freely.

(C) When the authority of the chieftans was still strong, on certain days and in order to celebrate their sacred rites they would convoke their subjects by sending heralds and messengers. Adorned according to their custom and painted with the juice of plants of different colors, all the men would assemble and especially the youth; women, on the other hand, came with neither paint nor adornment: the virgins were nude, and those who had known men had their private parts covered by short skirts. Both sexes had their arms, thighs, calves, and heels covered with the shells of certain snails which produced an agreeable noise upon any movement. They adorned their heads with garlands of flowers and different plants, otherwise being naked. Laden thus with shells, striking the ground with their feet, leaping, singing, and dancing, they greeted the chief, who received them seated at the threshold of his home, striking the drum with a stick.

□   □   □

Francisco López de Gómara, *Hispania victrix. Primera y segunda parte de la Historia general de las Indias, con todo el descubrimiento, y cosas notables que han acaecido desde que se ganaron hasta el año de 1551, con la conquista de México y de la Nueva España* (Zaragoza, 1552), in *Historiadores primitivos de Indias*, Enrique de Vedia, ed. Vol. 20, *Biblioteca de autores españoles* (Madrid: Rivadeneyra, 1887; reprinted Madrid, 1946), 173-74.[7]

Men and women were all very devout and observed many holy days; when the chief wished to celebrate the feast of his deity and principal idol, all would attend the service. They would adorn the idol very handsomely, then the priests would array themselves as in a chorus alongside the king, with the chief at the entrance of the temple, a drum at his side. The men would arrive, painted black, red, blue, and other colors, or adorned with branches and bearing garlands of flowers or feathers with shells on their arms and jingles on their legs. The women wore similar objects, but were nude and unpainted if virgins and wearing only breeches if married; they entered the temple dancing and singing to the sound of the shells. The chief would greet them with the drum as they arrived. Inside the temple all would induce vomiting by introducing a stick down the throat, in order to show the god that nothing bad remained in their stomachs. They would kneel and pray, resembling great birds producing an odd noise. Then many other women arrived bearing baskets of cakes on their heads, with quantities of roses, flowers and fragrant herbs on top. These women would surround those who were praying, and begin to sing a sort of old *romance* in praise of the god. All would rise to respond; with the end of the *romance* the music would change and they would intone another, again kneeling, in praise of the chief while offering bread to the idol. The priests would take the bread, blessing it and sharing it as we share the blessed host. In this way the service would end. People would save the bread for a year, and considered unfortunate the house which was without it, for that house would be defenseless against many dangers.

Areíto is like a revelry of Moors, who dance as they sing *romances* in praise of their kings and gods and in commemoration of victories and ancient and memorable occurrences; they have no other means of recounting their history. Many people dance in these *areítos*, which sometimes go on for a day and a night. The dancers end intoxicated on a certain native wine which is served them in the plaza.

Fray Ramón Revisited

Antonio de Herrera y Tordesillas, *Historia general de los hechos de los castellanos en las islas i tierra firme del mar océano*, 4 vols. (Madrid: Imprenta Real, 1601-1615), 1, 87 (Decade 1, Book 3, Chap. 4).[8]

[These sorcerers] . . . perpetrated a thousand deceptions in order to maintain those people in their blindness. The people knew nothing of their traditions except what they learned through songs. These they sang with an instrument made of thin and hollow wood, two feet long and one wide. The part that was played was shaped like a blacksmith's tongs and the other part like a club so that the instrument resembled a gourd with a long neck. This instrument was so loud that is could be heard for almost a league away, and to its sound the people sang their *romances*. It was played by the leading men, who learned to play it as children. They also sang to its accompaniment during dances where they became drunk.

[When the Admiral arrived as prophesied], they began to sing, and they sang for him in the style of their old *romances*, playing their drum as in such holidays as weddings and other celebrations, all holding hands, the leader singing and shouting. Men and women responded, sometimes men alone and at other times women alone and all drinking wine made of maize as well as other beverages until they fell drunk, something often seen among them; this fiesta would normally continue from morning until nightfall.

Notes

1. For a discussion of the chroniclers' and early historians' writings dealing with music and related subjects see Donald Thompson, "The *Cronistas de Indias* Revisited: Historical Reports, Archeological Evidence, and Literary and Artistic

Traces of Indigenous Music and Dance in the Greater Antilles at the Time of the *Conquista,*" *Latin American Music Review* 14, no. 2 (Fall/Winter 1993): 181-201.

2. Fray Ramón was commissioned by Christopher Columbus to report on the "beliefs and antiquities" of populations encountered during the Admiral's second exploratory voyage to the New World; the text is thus the earliest known description of New World indigenes and their ways. The *Relación* is known today in two versions, neither of which is original. It was included in Fernando Colón's biography of his father, the Admiral of the Ocean Seas, but this work has been lost. Existing is a translation to Italian dating from the end of the sixteenth century, from which the present excerpt is taken. The other known early version of Pané's text is a brief paraphrase to be seen in Peter Martyr's early sixteenth-century *Decades of the New World.* Although Fray Ramón's observations were made on the island of Hispaniola (today's Haiti and Dominican Republic) they are conventionally taken as valid for Puerto Rico as well.

3. Bartolomé de Las Casas, after joining the Dominican Order in Hispaniola, became a tireless champion of the aborigines, denouncing his Spanish compatriots' brutal treatment of them. His writings were based partly on observation and partly on the repetition and elaboration of the reports and writings of others, including Pané, and were often slanted to emphasize the similarity of native culture to the European. The present excerpt describes practices seen, reported, or imagined in Hispaniola, and have been extrapolated by other writers to cover Puerto Rico as well. The *Apologética historia,* existing in manuscript notes from the period 1527-1550 and with excerpts published in the nineteenth century, received its first publication in the edition cited here.

4. Oviedo, a Spanish colonial administrator on the South American mainland and in Hispaniola, arrived in the Antilles after the tide of conquest had passed westward and southward. For the Antilles, his work is based mainly on the preserved observations of earlier writers, and often incorporates material not relevant to this region at all. For this reason, much of it is open to question.

The present translation is based on the 1525 edition. However, most modern editions are derived from the 1851-1855 Madrid edition, which displays important variants. One of these affects the present text; "Tenían otra manera estas gentes . . ." (1525), translated here as "These people had a different way . . ." becomes "Tenían estas gentes una buena é gentil manera . . . ," often translated as ". . . a good and gracious way . . . ." There have been several other editions of Oviedo's text, including the following: José Amador de los Ríos, ed. (Madrid: Real Academia de la Historia, 3 vols. in 4, 1851-1855), the first complete edition; and in *Crónicas de Puerto Rico,* Eugenio Fernández Méndez, ed. (Río Piedras: Editorial Universitaria, 1981).

5. Pietro Martire D'Anghiera (ca. 1455-1526) is considered the first historian of the New World. Soldier, priest, courtier, and diplomat, he was named to the post of chief chronicler or historian to the Spanish Council of the Indies in 1520, and later, Secretary. Peter Martyr was never in America; acquainted with

Columbus, Vasco da Gama, Cortés, Magellan, Cabot, and Vespucci, he drew upon information obtained from these sources as well as from previous writings (including Pané) and documents passing through his hands at the Council of the Indies. His *Decades of the New World* were conceived as letters written to different persons over a period of more than thirty years beginning in 1494. The publication, republication, and translation of segments began in 1511, with a publication of the entire collection, in Latin, in 1530.

6. *Cemíes*, described in Decade 1, Book 9 and citing Fray Ramón Pané, as stuffed figures made of cotton. Stone *cemíes* have been unearthed throughout the region.

7. Gómara (1511-ca. 1560) was a priest and the chaplain to Hernando Cortés. Like Peter Martyr, he was never in America; Gómara's work was thus based on the writings of others and on information received from persons who had taken part in the *Conquista*. The accuracy of his historical writings has been challenged by many writers beginning with Las Casas, while the sources of many of his statements are immediately obvious even through his own glosses and ela-borations. It has been recognized that his writings record what was believed at the time regarding the subject; it is this fact which has justified his inclusion among the classic works of sixteenth-century Spanish historical writing.

8. This work by Herrera y Tordesillas (ca. 1549-1624) was commissioned by King Philip II and composed between 1601 and 1615; it is necessarily based on earlier reports and other documents, for the time of direct contact with the *Conquista* and persons active in it had long passed. Herrera's sources are evident: in the present excerpt, Fray Ramón Pané, perhaps by way of Las Casas. The same text may be seen in modern editions, including Madrid: Angel de Altolaguirre, ed. 2 vols, 1934, 2, 234-35; Asunción de Paraguay: Ed. Guaranía, 1944, 309.

2

Mountain, Plain, and Town:
Traditional Folk and Popular Music

The earliest scientific studies of Puerto Rican folk music were conducted in the early decades of the past century, with John Alden Mason's valuable text studies serving as the pioneer contribution.[1] Particularly since the 1950s the pace of research has increased considerably, with a number of academic theses and dissertations dealing with this subject submitted mainly to U.S. universities. Earlier knowledge is based on the writing of lay observers: travelers, ecclesiastics, historians, government functionaries, and an occasional Puerto Rican urban dweller concerned for the welfare of his barely known rural compatriots or amused by their customs.

One of the earliest and most often cited sources for nineteenth century folk life is Manuel Alonso's *El gíbaro* (1849). Although highly romanticized in the early *costumbrista* or nostalgic and regionalist fashion cultivated by Alonso and his fellow Puerto Rican students in Barcelona, Alonso's descriptions and those of Fr. Iñigo Abbad y Lasierra, including the excerpts included in this section, have been drawn upon by all later writers on musical subjects.

Little is known of the musical activities of Puerto Rico's slave population aside from the casual observations of visitors; two early English-language sources of interest can be seen in articles by Frank O. Gatell.[2] A governmental decree regarding the education and the pastimes of slaves, excerpted in this section, is a documented example of more official interest. With the abolition of slavery in 1873, many former slaves joined free blacks in the cities and towns as a new element in the labor force and in urban society. Luis Bonafoux's "El Carnaval en las Antillas," an excerpt of which is included in this section, is an extreme example of the post-emancipation racism which beset Puerto Rico; it is also an excellent example of the style of this skilled writer, whose work could be compared to that of H.L. Mencken, the Scourge of Baltimore. Like Mencken, Bonafoux employed a relentlessly ferocious style, applying it to all subjects regardless of the race or station of his victims.

A Dance

Fr. Íñigo Abbad y Lasierra, "Usos y costumbres de los habitantes de esta isla," in his *Historia geográfica, civil y política de la isla de San Juan Bautista de Puerto Rico* (Madrid: A. Valladares de Sotomayor, 1788), 279-80.[3]

The favorite entertainment of these islanders is dancing; they will organize a dance with no greater purpose than to simply pass the time, and seldom can dancing not be found in one home or another. The host invites his friends and the word travels throughout the entire region; hundreds of people who were not invited may appear from everywhere. As the houses are small few people fit inside; the rest remain beneath the house, which is elevated on columns, or in the yard, ascending the stairs when they wish to dance. To begin the dance some guests station themselves at the foot of the stairway with maracas, *güiro*, tambourine and a guitar or two; accompanied by these instruments they sing in honor of the host and his family, in a stylized kind of praise. In due course the host appears at the head of the stairway to welcome the invited guests and other persons, bidding them to enter; at the top of the stairs all embrace as if they had not seen one another for many years. The women seat themselves on benches and in hammocks; the men remain standing or squat on their heels while those who find no place within the house remain in the yard below.

People approach the dance floor singly or in couples as the men invite the women to dance; if a woman has no sandals (as is usually the case) she borrows another's. The man enters the room hat and all, and begins to perform twists and turns so fast that they seem to the woman like lightning flashes. The man places himself at one end of the room with his hat on the side of his head and his machete held in both hands across his shoulders. He does not leave his place nor does he make any movement other than stamping his feet with great speed and great force. If he happens to be dancing on a loose board so much the better, for the sound of his bare feet can then drown out that of the singers and instrumentalists. When he or some other man wishes to compliment a woman dancer he takes off his hat and places it on her head. Sometimes so many hats are placed on a woman's head that she cannot carry them all; she then holds some in her hands or under her arms. When she is tired of dancing she retires from the floor with a curtsy and returns the hats to their owners, each of whom then gives her a coin, a half *real*; this act is referred to as *dar la gala*. If a man wishes to dance with a woman who is already dancing with someone else he must ask permission. Arguments often break out over this point, and as every man carries justice in his hands, dances usually end in machete fights.

During the dance, slaves appear bearing bowls of a thick refreshment made of flour, milk, and honey to serve the guests, along with liquor and smoking tobacco. Those who become tired lie in the hammocks or freely withdraw to the pallets which are found in the inner room of the house. Others retire to their own homes to return another day, for these dances usually last a whole week. When one group of dancers leaves the floor another takes its place, and the dance continues day and night with people traveling two or three leagues just to take part in a party whose music, singing, and din of stamping feet would leave the strongest head giddy for a long time.

These dances take place mainly at the Christmas season, during Carnival, during village festivals, and in connection with weddings, whose celebration begins two months before the event. The birth or death of a baby is also observed with a dance; in the latter case the dance may continue until the stench of the body can no longer be tolerated although preparations may have been made for a party of many days' duration. Such parties are organized and paid for by the child's godparents.

Slave Life

"Reglamento. Sobre la educación, trato y ocupaciones que deben dar á sus esclavos los dueños y mayordomos en esta Isla. Núm. 225. Puerto Rico y agosto 12 de 1826. Miguel de la Torre," in *Prontuario de disposiciones oficiales*, Francisco Ramos, ed. (Puerto Rico: Imprenta de González, 1866), 1.[4]

Chapter VII. On Recreation

Art. 1. Owners shall permit their slaves to entertain themselves and enjoy virtuous forms of recreation on holidays (after having heard mass and attended their lessons in Christian doctrine) within the plantation and without mixing with slaves of other plantations, in an open place in sight of their owners, managers, and overseers.

Art. 2. These amusements and diversions are to be carried out by men and women separately: the men in such contests of strength as stone hurling, pole throwing, ball games, and bowls; the women, separately, at forfeits and similar activities. All, the men and women separately, may dance to their skin-headed drums[5] and other instruments used by *bozales*[6] or to guitars or vihuelas as played by *criollos*.[7]

Art. 3. These diversions may continue only until sunset or until the call to prayer.

Art. 4. Owners and managers are especially charged with exercising the greatest vigilance in preventing the intermixing of the sexes, excessive drinking, and the participation of free blacks and of slaves from other plantations.

Puerto Rican Dances and
Native Musical Instruments

Manuel A. Alonso, "Bailes de Puerto Rico," in his *El gíbaro* (Barcelona: Juan Oliveres, 1849), 58-67.[8]

Two kinds of dances are known in Puerto Rico. One kind belongs to society, and these simply echo the European social dances. The others, called *bailes de garabato*, are distinctive to Puerto Rico although they appear to me to be derived from Spanish dances intermixed with those of the island's primitive inhabitants.[9] Some African dances are known as well, introduced by the blacks of those regions, but they have never become widespread in Puerto Rico. These are called *bailes de bomba*, after the instrument which provides their music. The most frequently seen social dances are the *contradanza* and the waltz. The *contradanza* is the Spanish dance of the same name, preserved much better in Puerto Rico than in Spain itself; its figures display the variety which originally marked the *contradanza*, while its steps acquire greater charm with the natural grace of the daughters of the tropics. It is impossible to follow with the eye the motion of one of those dark beauties of languid glance, slender waist, and tiny foot without feeling his heart expand to the point of leaping from his breast. The *contradanza americana* is the most expressive dance imaginable; it is truly a poem of passion and of beguiling visions: in a word, the story of a charmed love.[10]

The dance begins. . . . The enchantress is invited to the floor by an admirer who finds his way to his beloved despite all obstacles. The figures of the *contradanza* dramatically symbolize restraints to some (the young men), but safety to others (the young ladies). At the beginning the dancers hesitatingly approach each other; they separate; they again approach each other, each time lingering longer. They take each other's hands; the young man touches his beloved's arms, her waist. Finally united in the dance, the couple surrenders to pleasure along with all of their friends, who are also celebrating the joy of the union of two beings in love. Oh, daughters of my homeland! No one can equal thee in dancing; no other countenance pours forth that torrent of pure ardor that is thine nor that enchanting voluptuousness which is native to our climate alone! The music which contributes not a little to the enchantment of the *contradanza* is a mélange of suggestions: now melancholy, mournful and sentimental; now cheerful, witty and boisterous. This music is a product of the island itself, and composers sometimes use known folk melodies, finding a pretext in some more or less celebrated event to compose a piece which will then bear their name. I have known musicians widely recognized in Europe who do not like this music. In my presence such a musician once played a very pretty *contradanza* on the piano, and I could not help thinking that the way he played it would make it impossible for anyone to like it. Then a young Cuban lady played it who was no more than half skilled as a pianist. She had hardly finished when the European musician asked me: "Do you know why I enjoyed hearing this young lady play? Imagine a foreigner who speaks Spanish perfectly. Finding himself in Madrid he is asked to read aloud one of those witty pieces written in Andalusian dialect by Rubí or another of our fine poets. I am sure that he would not at all enjoy dealing with the alteration, elimination or adding of syllables or the use of odd words and other strange things that he would find in the text. Well, then; if our foreigner were taken to the theater of an evening to see the same play performed by good actors he would die laughing and would applaud like a fool. Something similar has just happened to me; in order to really understand the *contradanza* I had to hear one played by someone from the Antilles."

"And now would you like to play it again?" "No, indeed! For all of my rules and for all of my experience, I should find myself in the situation of the foreigner whom I described before, if he were to try to recite the Andalusian piece again!"

As is the case everywhere, in Puerto Rico the waltz is the inseparable companion of the *contradanza* and is regarded as its obligatory
sequel; the young lady who accepts an invitation to dance a *contradanza*
knows that she will then have to waltz with the same partner. The
rigodón is also well known in Puerto Rico: calm, serene and aristocratic,
it retains under the tropical sun the same qualities which it possesses in
the arctic cold of Europe. All of the other dances which have had some
acceptance in Europe have also arrived in Puerto Rico and have lasted
briefly or for some time depending upon the pleasure with which they
are received. Thus over the years we have seen the galop, the mazurka,
the *britano*, the *cotillón*, the polka, etc.

As far as their rules are concerned, these social dances are almost
the same in Puerto Rico as those that I have seen in Europe except for a
few changes which are not distinctive enough to impart to them a particular character. Among these is the peculiarity which I have mentioned: that the waltz is considered a supplement to the *contradanza*,
which thus governs it in the choice of partners. It seems to me that this
custom must be rooted in some older practice: a sign of the pleasure
which a couple has enjoyed in the *contradanza*, a sign which through
repetition became a law sanctioned by use. Like other such laws it has
not failed to cause discomfort. If the reader doubts this, let him imagine
an attractive and cultured young lady who has accepted the impetuous
invitation of some hopeful but inexperienced fumbler who becomes red
as a berry on addressing her. Upon touching her hand and observing the
agitation of her breast his ears ring and he stumbles. The girl cannot
rebuke him because the laws of good manners are inflexible on this
point; it would be an unpardonable offense to anyone still in the age of
new and unknown experiences. The music begins, and the couple commences a motion similar to that of the beam of a mill as it crushes the
grain: one end rises as the other falls and vice versa. Our dancers collide;
they step on each other's feet; they grapple. Bruised all over, they arrive
at the end of the *contradanza*. Just as the young lady begins to compose
herself after such a misfortune the instruments are heard again, and she
must resume her martyrdom, now in the waltz.

I shall say nothing of the young man who is called upon to dance
with a cousin of his beloved, or a friend of his little sister, or a young
lady recommended by his mother or by the hostess, although I could
describe this at length. However, I wish not to because I greatly cherish
the fair sex, including even those representatives to whom the adjective
does not apply; therefore let us proceed to another subject.

Placement in the *contradanza* is also of the greatest importance. Unless there are very strong reasons for doing so, no one wants another to precede him in the figures, once places have been taken. This seems correct to me, for it acknowledges that there should be equal and mutual respect among honorable persons. Only one couple, the first in line, begins to dance; as they move toward the far end of the hall they are followed by the other couples in the strictest order. This is contrary to what we have seen in other places, where no particular placement is preferred and everyone begins to dance at the same time. However, that way causes confusion which lasts as long as the music itself. Among the diversity of figures which may be used, no dancer may stray from the figure set by the first couple, and even these may change the figure only as they return to their starting place.

This is the only difference among the social dances of the more comfortable classes in Puerto Rico; in all other aspects they have no reason to envy the finest dances to be seen anywhere else (with the exception of royal courts), for their participants manifest all of the necessary conditions of grace and elegance, while their attire and the decor of the locales display splendor and good taste. Especially dazzling are the dances given by institutions and organizations whenever some occasion merits the great expense which must be borne. Individual persons also compete in offering dances of great splendor, for dancing provides the island's principal entertainment.

As I have said, there are several *bailes de garabato*, which originated in a mixture of Spanish and native Indian dances. The resulting dances clearly display the style of one or another precursor. Thus anyone would recognize in the *cadenas,* and the *fandanguillo* the deterioration of the *seguidillas* and the *fandango*; one also sees something of the *zapateado* in the *sonduro,* along with a great deal of that frantic dizziness which seemed to transfigure people who spent entire days seated on their heels. In addition to the *fandanguillo*, the *cadenas* and the *sonduro* or *matatoros* are found the *seis* and the *caballo*, which complete the repertory of *bailes de garabato*. The first mentioned is the Spanish *fandango*, although in the name of truth I must point out that while the *contradanza* has benefited greatly the *fandango* has suffered, and not a little. Its steps are executed with much less ease and grace while the dancers' feet do not slide across the floor as smoothly as might be desired. Their bodies maintain a rigidity which in addition to appearing affected does not suit the mood and style of the music. Their arms, which can add so much charm to any pose, sometimes become bothersome appendages which dancers do not know where to place. In a word, the *fandanguillo* is a poorly adapted transplant.

The *cadenas* is derived from the *seguidillas*, but not as any malformed and feeble imitation. Instead it represents a brisk and vigorous renewal, which I have compared to a lovely girl of mixed race. This is the most animated and eye-catching of all of these dances. One or more groups of up to four couples each may take part, executing an agreed upon number of attractive figures. These display such precision and such poise that no one would wish to know the stiff and cold dancers of the *fandanguillo*; here they swiftly cross in different directions, joining themselves to form attractive groups and instantly changing positions an infinite number of times, always returning to their starting point. Nothing could depict the elated merriment of the country folk as well as the *cadenas*. Its music is simple but very lively, while the song which accompanies it is highly expressive; it is not possible to render the song texts any higher praise than to point out that many are *seguidillas* which I have heard in Spain. Without knowing it, the *jíbaros* sometimes sing verses by Iglesias and by other equally celebrated authors.

The *sonduro* is a kind of *zapateado* but marked by such bursts of enthusiasm that not only does the couple in the center of the floor dance but everyone else in the room moves rhythmically as well. The planks of the floor creak, while the deafening drumming of bare feet covered by a half inch of thick and leathery skin, or shod with nailed sandals, carries farther in the silence of the night than the instruments, which are rather loud themselves. All of this noise is produced by pairs of feet belonging to the men, for the women have no part in it. As dancers tire they are relieved by others; for this reason it is not uncommon to hear this drumming continue for such a long time that it could not possibly be produced by a single person.

Strictly speaking the *seis* should be danced by six couples, although I have seen it danced by many more. Women and men place themselves in facing rows; they cross several times, stamp their feet a little at certain times in the music, and end by waltzing as after the *contradanza*. After the *cadenas* the *seis* is preferred among the *bailes de garabato*, for it is neither deafening like the *sonduro* nor dull like the *fandanguillo* and the *caballo*.

In the *caballo*, couples face each other but crossing, with each lady standing beside the other lady's partner. The dance calls for some simple steps lacking variety, in which couples cross and change partners without ever touching hands; for a foreigner this dance would offer little grace or interest.

The native musical instruments also merit description. A complete orchestra is formed by a *bordonúa*, a *tiple*, a *cuatro*, a *carracho*, and a *maraca*. The *bordonúa* is a guitar of large size and rough construction, sometimes fashioned with no more tools than a knife or a dagger. Several varieties of wood are used, except that the top is always of *yagrumo*, one of the fairest woods known as well as one of the lightest in weight. The *tiple* is exactly the same, except that it is much smaller. The *cuatro* represents an average size between them, but is different because its middle section ends in two angles near the neck, unlike the other shape which is rounded, as in the *bordonúa*. The *carracho, güiro,* or *calabazo* is a large dried gourd with deep grooves carved across it; over this instrument a stiff wooden stick is softly or loudly scraped. A hole is made in the side opposite the grooves so that the sound might be more intense. With the instrument in the left hand the stick is held in the right and moved as I have described. The *maraca* is a *jigüera* pierced by a stick and containing a few small hard seeds. When shaken by the right hand, grasping the part of the protruding stick which serves as a handle, it produces a sound with which performers accompany the other instruments.

The rules of the *bailes de garabato* are rigorously followed, and no participant is excused from conscientiously observing them. Although these dances are most appropriate for people of the lower class and for the country folk as I have said, I have sometimes seen very distinguished persons taking part in them. Treading on another man's foot, a shove, a lover's jealousy, a spectator's smile and similar incidents not infrequently cause dances to end in knife battles. On the other hand, in the absence of these conditions the people oblige and defer to one another with the greatest openness, always favoring the visitor over persons of the neighborhood. In a word, those good people observe all of the niceties which are compatible with their class, their customs, and their level of education.

Such are the *bailes de garabato*. The dances of the blacks of Africa and of the natives of Curaçao do not merit inclusion here; although they are seen in Puerto Rico they have never become widespread. I mention them because due to their number they add to the great variety of dances which a foreigner might see on a single island and even without leaving a specific town. It would be useless for me to attempt to prove that this variety has resulted from Puerto Rico's geographical location, which has attracted persons from many nations each of which has introduced customs that more or less take root depending on the influence which each has exerted. I conclude, then, that except for the public balls and grand productions of the European theaters which we cannot have because our theater is closed during the greater part of the year and because I doubt that anyone in Puerto Rico wishes to face ruin through contracting companies which have caused the greatest impresarios to fail, where dances are concerned there is no reason for us to envy any country in the world.

Carnival

Luis Bonafoux, "El Carnaval en las Antillas," in his *Ultramarinos* (Madrid: Imprenta y Fundición de M. Tello, 1882), 1-8.[11]

If here in Old Europe, which boasts of knowing beauty and style, we are not surprised that most of the public annually abandons itself to the supreme pleasure of twirling about wearing vulgar masks and motley costumes while roaming the streets, later to enjoy the pleasant diversion of humiliating others with pranks of doubtful taste, it should not surprise us that in America, always late in reflecting the achievements of European progress, certain customs are still preserved from time immemorial: customs poorly adapted to the most rudimentary principles of urbanity, civilization, and style. As we observe the slow but certain disappearance of these Carnival bacchanals in Spain, we hope that certain customs which we hesitate to call savage only because such a description seems too tolerant, might also gradually disappear in the Spanish Antilles as well.

In such places, blessed by extremely prodigious nature, the customs of the inhabitants have been shaped by nature's own exuberance, an exuberance which is born in the inhabitants themselves. But just as their impenetrable forests and impassable underbrush have succumbed to man's constant labor, so are their ancient customs succumbing to the labor of progress. Here in Spain we view with disdain the vestiges of celebrations which although still alive have been fading away; there, in America, we observe with shock and pain the revels of a savage and untamed rabble.

During Carnival, confusion and tumult reign. Crowds of men, women, and children roam the streets in the small hours of the morning, violently awakening anyone so foolish as to sleep during such joyous times. First the sleeper hears the harsh and disagreeable screeching of the inharmonious *güícharo*,[12] the island's principal musical instrument; next a window of his house is broken by a stone skillfully hurled by a member of the "organizing committee." This act provokes the laughter of the proprietor of the corner cigar store, who emerges barefoot and in his underdrawers, enjoying his eleventh cup of coffee as he greets the happy throng. It also pleases the night watchman, exhilarated in shirt-sleeves and silk hat, who cries "Two fifteen, and crowds in the streets!"

The people who are referred to as *of color* also celebrate Carnival, with dancing being the main entertainment of a people who are born with the right foot ready to dance and who die with the left one in the same position. Merry and lubricious couples surrender with the licentiousness of satyrs to an orgiastic dance, called the *merengue* for its exquisite titillation. There one sees the impudent and sensual mulatta: her hair undone, her lips compressed by the paroxysm of pleasure, her eyes soft and moist, her palpitating bosom threatening to escape from its tenuous and indiscreet barrier, her hips in lascivious undulations: breathless, sweaty, ardent, thinking only of pleasure and living only for pleasure. Meanwhile, in some untilled and filthy wilderness, blacks of both sexes abandon themselves to pleasure in a delicious dance. With the men almost naked and the women covered by banana leaves and all shouting imprecations to the heavens, they dance around three or four black and famous musicians who with their *bombas* produce a gentle sound: about as gentle as cannon shots! Soon the dust fills the air and a delicate perfume of male goat pervades the atmosphere; the imprecations are steadily more violent and the jungle cries more shrill as the *bomba* continues to sound. All is *jayuya*, as the blacks say: a perfect delight.

The rage for disguises is everywhere indescribable: even the blacks wear masks! Celebrants organize processions of *vejigantes*,[13] whose favorite prank is to attack the first person they meet with great bladders, while shouting such verses as "*Vejigante la boya! Pan y cebolla!*"

The *high life*[14] of the island also takes part in these processions; they attack homes, plunder the families, appropriate the *mofongo* prepared ahead for the day's celebrations, steal the avocado salad and the dessert and even enter the interior quarters so that their joy might be widespread and so that all might together proclaim "What a delightful fiesta!" In this way is Carnival celebrated in the Antilles.

Folk Instruments and the Decline of Traditional Dances

Francisco del Valle Atiles, *El campesino puertorriqueño: sus condicio-nes físicas, intelectuales y morales, causas que las determinan y medios para mejorarlas* (San Juan: Tipo. de José González Font, 1887), 111-14.[15]

Let us speak, however briefly, of rustic musical instruments. The *maraca* is a kind of rattle of Antillean Indian origin, which by its name and by the noise which it produces might be compared with the *matraca*,[16] an uncouth and primitive representative of the musical instruments of almost all uncivilized lands. The *güiro* is an unpleasant instrument for ears not accustomed to the dry clatter caused by scraping its grooved surface; there are also derivatives of the guitar and the bandurria which invite our consideration. These include the *tiple*, a little five-stringed guitar displaying the inexplicable peculiarity of having its first and fifth strings tuned the same, which produces an anomalous combination of notes. The *cuatro* has four double courses of strings, and is tuned and played like the bandurria; the *bordonúa* has six strings and the *vihuela* up to ten, for in this matter the imagination of the instrument maker enters into play. The construction of these instruments obeys no rational artistic concept; their little material value requires that the *jíbaros* themselves must make them, usually using inappropriate tools. It would be interesting to determine the process of degeneration which our national stringed instruments have experienced in this province. The concepts which govern the construction of guitars and *bandurrias* survive in them, but the lack of tools to make them in the same forms that were brought from Spain has caused imperfections to occur.

As imperfect as they are, they can produce agreeable sounds. Skilled hands draw pleasant melodies from these crude instruments despite the serious difficulties which they must certainly present. Players exist who with surprising mastery display their skill in producing amazing melodies, especially on the *cuatro*. Accompanying himself with these crude instruments the *jíbaro* sings his languid and erotic ballads, or during the Christmas season his animated villancicos.

Such a reduced orchestra serves the *jíbaro* for his dances, and it is a pity that some of the dance forms are falling into oblivion. The *seis*, perhaps named for the seises who danced before the altar in some forgotten Christian ritual, is a figure dance of some grace. It is regrettable that it is losing its memory of such old figure dances as the *danza española*, today supplanted by the sensual *merengue*,[17] to which the *seis* has also become accommodated.

The *sonduro*, the *cadenas, caballos, puntillanto, fandanguillo* and perhaps other types which have not been completely forgotten are nevertheless being relegated to an unjustified oblivion.

The so-called *caballo* requires that the dancers execute dizzying waltz figures; in the *sonduro* the footwork must be very loud; at times the dancers would attach steel plates to their shoes in order to make more noise. *Cadenas* is a dance of very attractive figures and pretty music, associated with song; the *puntillanto* is a sort of *zorcico* with loud footwork, of highly agreeable music and appearing to combine ternary and binary meters for a beautiful effect. This is still another figure dance which is hardly remembered in some regions of the interior.

Modern dances tend to displace all of these older forms. In society, the figure dances are forgotten and the same thing is happening in the country, endangering the very character of the old dances, for in the final analysis, dancing has its spiritual aspect in addition to being a sensible form of exercise. Dance and its associated music have expressed the most elevated of emotions: religious emotion, emotions of love, warlike emotions; but today they express only the passion of love, and when represented by modern steps they become rather brutal.

We do not mean that this must always occur whenever modern steps are danced, but one should not ignore the danger of it occurring. It is possible to dance the *merengue* correctly and innocently, but in this dance are united a number of circumstances against which it is best to be warned. . . . Let the *danza* be danced, certainly, but not so exclusively that it supersedes other dances more beautiful and more spiritual.

A Professional Musician's View

Julio Carlos de Arteaga, "Breve memoria sobre los cantos populares de Puerto-Rico," *Ilustración Musical Hispano-americana* (Barcelona) 6, no. 129 (30 May 1893): 74; 6, no. 130 (15 June 1893): 82-83.[18]

Foreigners and peninsular Spaniards who visit Puerto Rico for the first time are surprised not only by the islanders' musical ear, a trait which is typical of many regions of Spanish America, but also by the rhythmic and melodic qualities of their music. Although Puerto Rican music is not always completely original, it is distinguished by a species of dance music which is exclusively Puerto Rican. Called simply the *danza*, it has been cultivated in Puerto Rico (and only in Puerto Rico) since time immemorial. Also of interest is the monotonous and plaintive quality of the island's folk songs, especially those which express the character of the true son of the soil: a character both timid and persistent in the amorous relationships which frequently provide the subjects of such songs.

In order to understand the most salient characteristics of Puerto Rican song, rhythm and harmony, one must take into account that the first settlers had been taught music by their Spanish ancestors, who would certainly never have expected their songs to become transformed here, acquiring through the passing of time and the effect of climate a definitely tropical character, to some degree appropriate for the island. It must be understood that similar cases have occurred in other regions of Spanish America, but it should be noted as a curiosity that Puerto Rican folk song has not completely forgotten its roots in the Iberian provinces. This is unlike the situation in Cuba, Puerto Rico's sister island, nor in Venezuela, Colombia, or Chile, whose music is more exclusively American. In these countries the primitive Indian sentiment is sensed in the rhythms and the melodies of their folk song. The essentially Puerto Rican folk songs are based on modern European harmony, which supports my statement that they are derived from characteristics peculiar to the provinces of peninsular Spain.

The character of these songs is thus southern, but different from the South European. The plaintive trait in Puerto Rican song is not marked by extended singing on a single note, as in Andalusian song, for example, nor do we find those long repeated trills or coloraturas on the sixth scale degree in minor mode, as in Andalusian song. The melodic flow of Puerto Rican song is more economical. On the other hand, as regards the accompaniment, and particularly regarding instrumental passages, Puerto Rican music is much more lavish in its ornamentation. Worthy of attention are the improvisations which the *gíbaro* produces on the accompanying instrument known as the *cuatro*.[19] These improvisations provide a kind of musical dialogue, alternating with the sung couplets. These strokes of inventiveness might be called Puerto Rican counterpoint, if such a term were not too presumptuous, because the *gíbaro* occasionally displays so much skill at this intuitive musical game that if he were to receive instruction he might devote himself to the study of the difficult science of academic counterpoint. More than once (and this is no exaggeration) I have been reminded of the variations composed by French and German harpsichordists of the sixteenth century, on hearing the improvisations of the *gíbaro*, solemnly hunched over his inseparable *cuatro*.

Regarding the inner feelings which move the *gíbaro* to play this favored instrument, it appears that agitation and restlessness rule his spirit. This is in surprising contrast to his habitual way of life, which could not be quieter, more apathetic or more lethargic as regards spiritual life, given the level of ignorance in which he lives.

As for the modes and harmonies used in the songs of the *gíbaros*, I might add that although certain signs of Spanish origin are noted, songs and passages in minor mode are free of the Moorish minor: that mode which is so widely applied in the Andalusian provinces. As is well known, the main characteristic of the Moorish minor is its alteration of the sixth and seventh scale degrees in the descending minor mode.

Puerto Rican folk song is often laid out like the old plainchant, that is, within the melodic compass of a fifth (tonic to dominant), with an occasional use of the lower leading tone and frequent employment of the sixth scale degree. Thus the only difference in these two types of melody, although it is a great difference indeed, is the appearance of the leading tone in the *gíbaro* mode.

But what is most peculiar in Puerto Rican music is the accompaniment of a certain dance called the *seis*, a name without doubt deriving from the fact that it should, strictly speaking, be danced by six couples. The *seis* is the cotillion of Puerto Rico, both because of its excessive length (it seems interminable) and because it is usually the dance which ends the ball. This type of music is very characteristic of the Puerto Rican peasant, who after an evening of dancing and drinking begins to feel their effect and surrenders to a kind of motion which becomes steadily more unbridled and disorderly. The *zapateo*[20] plays an important part in this dance.

Three aspects of this music are worthy of note: (1) the constant use of duple meter; (2) the frequent use of triplets, either within a beat or spread over an entire measure; and (3) final cadences which frequently end on the dominant in root position or in second inversion, with the supertonic in the bass.

Also worthy of note is the constant alternation of duple and triple meter, which might be combined in a single measure of 5/4[21] except for the inconvenience which it would cause; for this reason it would have to be transcribed in 6/4. However, as neither notation is known to most of the island's musicians, this would mean that they would not be able to read their own music.

Puerto Rican composers, like their peninsular Spanish teachers and predecessors, are fond of triplet figures, especially in eighth-note values.

They will often tie the last triplet of a group to the first of the following group. This device, not so frequently encountered in Spanish songs as is the use of triplets generally, endows Puerto Rican song with a certain languor or carelessness characteristic of tropical countries. This is often encountered in the *danza*, which is the musical form most characteristic of the island.

Songs not associated with dancing are of little importance in Puerto Rico, for they are with few exceptions derived from opera and zarzuela, theatrical forms often presented and highly favored there. In any case, these songs are more directly associated with European music. For these reasons I have decided to provide a general view of the dances which accompany singing but not of their texts, which are usually nonsensical or of the worst taste. Very seldom are these texts important as poetry, as the reader could easily determine if he had several examples before him. For this reason I have limited my brief study to a very small number of songs, believing that I have addressed these Puerto Rican folk songs with the attention which their scarcity merits: that is, limiting my observations to the songs' origin and to the specific qualities of their harmony and rhythm.

The predilection of Puerto Rican composers for the minor mode was noted above, but this predilection does not prevent modulation to the relative major, from which there is a certain difficulty in parting. However, there are highly stylized modern *danzas*, both with and without texts (in the former cases the texts are highly acceptable and even poetic), such as the *danzas* of Juan Morel Campos, the most celebrated Puerto Rican composer today. Following him in popularity are Arturo Pasarell and Mariano Casanovas. Today, public taste has changed greatly, finding in these modern *danzas* harmonies which if not rich, neither are they trivial as were those of the island's old songs. They contain melodies not lacking in inventiveness as well as the refined rhythms not found in the songs mentioned above, which have rightly fallen into oblivion.

A Folk Dance

Manuel Fernández Juncos, "El seis enojao," *Semana* (San Juan), 13 May 1922: 11.

To be spelled correctly, the name of this popular dance lacks a "d," for it should be *seis enojado*.[22] However, it is pronounced *enojao* in the countryside, where it was very popular in the past and where it is still danced today. This is perhaps the only figure dance which survives among our simple folk, and like almost all such dances it is the mute expression of a love poem, in this case seasoned with the spice of jealousy.

As the orchestra commences the cheerful and rhythmical strains of the *seis* a young couple detaches itself from the crowd. They smile happily as they link their arms and begin to dance the *seis*, with all of the enthusiasm of their youth and displaying all of the grace and creole elegance which God has bestowed upon them.

They happily dance to the best of their abilities; the applause of the bystanders encourages them, and their dancing becomes even more lively. At this moment the young man glances more seriously at the crowd, as if to better acknowledge their applause. He stares at a pretty girl in the crowd and nods his head slightly. His partner is conscious of this but feigns indifference, although a cloud of displeasure passes over her face. The couple continues to dance, the young lady less enthusiastically. As the dance takes them before the pretty *jíbara* again, the young man stares at her more intensely; his feet stumble and he loses the beat.

His partner then makes a gesture of anger. Disengaging herself, she takes a position before him as if to avoid all contact. They continue in this fashion, the young man in pursuit of his partner, but always to the rhythm of the *seis*. He makes conciliatory gestures as if to proclaim his innocence in order to appease her, while she displays her displeasure through subtle gestures. However, and in spite of her jealousy, she surrenders again to the music's appeal and to love's enslaving charm. Gradually, and in response to her partner's display of surrender, her face loses its shadow of displeasure although she hides it from him lest he become vain in his triumph.

But the young man has had enough of her resistance, and begins to show displeasure himself. His dancing lags behind and finally stops entirely. The young lady, no longer angry, turns toward him with open arms, but he rejects the invitation. Now the dance is reversed, with the young man angry and his partner entreating.

But soon his anger subsides as she turns her head to look at him invitingly. Finally, as the music becomes *allegro*, they again link their arms to the applause of the observers, and the music suddenly stops. The young man directs a courtly poem, called a *bomba*,[23] to his partner, and is roundly applauded by all. The musicians then play an animated *allegro*, and the *seis* becomes generalized as all the couples take happily to the floor.

None of today's new dances is more expressive and more delightful than the *seis enojao* of our colonial times. Why, then, in the Puerto Rican countryside is it being banished to the shadows of oblivion?

Notes

1. "Porto Rican Folk-Lore: Décimas, Christmas Carols, Nursery Rhymes, and Other Songs," Aurelio M. Espinosa, ed., *Journal of American Folklore* 31, no. 121 (July-September 1918): 289-450.

2. "Puerto Rico in the 1830s; the Journal of Edward Bliss Emerson," *The Americas* 16, no. 1 (July 1959): 62-75; "Puerto Rico Through New England Eyes," *Journal of Inter-American Studies* 1, no. 3 (July 1959): 281-92.

3. Abbad's account, the earliest known description of social dancing in the settled colony, has often been reprinted: as *Historia geográfica, civil y natural de la isla de Puerto Rico*, José Julián de Acosta y Calbo, ed. (Puerto Rico: Imprenta y Librería de Acosta, 1866); ed. with extensive notes by Isabel Gutiérrez del Arroyo (Río Piedras: Ediciones de la Universidad de Puerto Rico, 1959); as vol. 1 of Pedro Tomás de Córdoba, *Memorias geográficas, históricas, económicas y estadísticas de la isla de Puerto Rico*, 6 vols. ([San Juan], 1831-1833), reprinted San Juan: Instituto de Cultura Puertorriqueña, 1968.

4. Miguel de la Torre, Governor General of Puerto Rico, 1822-1837.

5. *bombas de pellejo*.

6. Slaves not born in America but imported directly from Africa.

7. Native-born persons.

8. Manuel A. Alonso (1822-1889) was a member of a group of young Puerto Rican writers whose work, begun as students in Barcelona, marked the beginning of the literary movement known as *costumbrismo*, a regionalist expression which drew attention, somewhat sentimentalized, to the life and ways of the Puerto Rican country folk. *El gíbaro*, an anthology of Alonso's previously published essays and poetry plus new material, has often been reprinted, usually with the modern spelling *jíbaro* in reference to rural dwellers: for example, an enl. 2d ed., 2 vols., San Juan, 1882-1883; F. Manrique Cabrera and José A. Torres Morales, eds., Río Piedras, 1949; and numerous reprints of excerpts.

9. A supposition not supported by research, although Alonso's view was accepted and repeated by influential folklorist María Cadilla de Martínez, "La música popular de Puerto Rico," *Puerto Rico Ilustrado* (San Juan), 4 June 1938: 22, 117-21.

10. A footnote at p. 48 of the second edition offers Alonso's comment of some 40 years later: "The Puerto Rican *danza* of today is a very different thing; only we oldtimers remember how it was danced in 1842."

11. Luis Bonafoux (1855-1918) was born in France and spent his formative years in Puerto Rico. Active as a jounalist, novelist, biographer, and poet both in Spain and in Puerto Rico at different periods of his life, Bonafoux was noted for the elegantly vitriolic style of his journalistic essays in particular. The present essay, originally published in *La Unión* (Madrid) in 1879, aroused such indignation in Puerto Rico that the author's next visit to the island was cut short as he fled for his life. He never returned, making his home successively in Madrid, Paris, and London.

12. Or *güiro*, the familiar scraped gourd.

13. Masked and fantastically garbed figures, particularly associated with the celebration of St. James the Apostle (Santiago) in the island's predominantly black regions.

14. Original in English.

15. Excerpts of this prize-winning study of the Puerto Rican peasant's health, diet, illnesses, customs, and state of education have often been reprinted, for example in *Crónicas de Puerto Rico*, Eugenio Fernández Méndez, ed. (1957), 2nd ed. (Río Piedras: Editorial Universitaria, 1969), 508-40.

16. Probably a cog-rattle or ratchet, although the word has also referred to clappers, enclosed rattles, and other sound producers.

17. The reference is not to the *merengue* known today, associated mainly with the Dominican Republic, but to the second and freely danced section of the *danza puertorriqueña*. The term was also used to refer to the Puerto Rican *danza* as a whole.

18. Arteaga (1865-1923) was an admired pianist and organist born in Mayagüez and trained in Paris and New York City. His successful performing and teaching career was developed internationally, with periods of residence in San Juan, Ponce, Havana, and New York City. The present article, one of many examples of Arteaga's writing, was awarded honorable mention in a contest of folk song studies sponsored by the *Ilustración Musical Hispano-americana*.

19. Author's note: The *cuatro* is a plucked-string instrument the number of whose strings is indicated by its name. Its construction is crude because of the scarcity of tools available to the *gíbaro* in fashioning it. Its tuning varies, but it is usually tuned in fourths.

20. Rapid and sonorous footwork.

21. A very questionable point. More likely is hemiola, the alternation or interplay of 3/4 and 6/8 meters, observed in folk and popular music throughout Spain and Latin America and in some other regions, as well as in concert music by Mozart, Haydn, Beethoven, Brahms, Tchaikovsky and many other composers.

22. Angry, cross, irritated.

23. Not to be confused with the *bomba* dance of the coastal regions, named for the *bomba* drum and associated with African survivals in Puerto Rican folk music.

3

NINETEENTH-CENTURY
MUSICAL LIFE

Concert life, lyric theater, church music, military music, and amateur
music making in nineteenth-century Puerto Rico were centered on the
towns. San Juan, the north-coast administrative seat of the Spanish colonial government, along with Ponce on the south coast, displayed signs of
musical vitality and similar adornments of culture early in the century
and in fact developed a serious rivalry in these and other matters. This
rivalry was nicely symbolized by a celebrated orchestral duel taking
place in 1882 and described in this section. Puerto Rico found a place in
the itineraries of touring opera and zarzuela companies early in the century, while receiving the visits of individual artists ranging from cellists
to ventriloquists. A most welcome pair of visitors were pianist Louis Moreau Gottschalk and the adolescent soprano Adelina Patti, who spent a
year touring the island in 1857-1858, at a time when many towns besides
San Juan and Ponce were developing an interest in concert music and
the lyric stage. The San Juan Municipal Theater has experienced many
periods of distinction and as many periods of distress since its inauguration in 1832, providing a stage for acrobats, magicians, ventriloquists,
and musicians including Gottschalk and Patti; one of the venerable theater's periods of distress is humorously described herein by a foremost
writer of the period. Toward the end of the century, music in commercial
advertising took its place alongside gas lights and the trolley as signs of
progress. Its characteristics are described in a recent article resulting
from new research.

A Visiting Virtuoso Honored:
Gottschalk in Ponce

"Baile," *El Fénix* (Ponce), 5 December 1857: 3.

The dance which took place on Saturday evening in honor of Mr. Gottschalk and Miss Patti in the home of Don Jorge Lohse, U.S. and Norwegian Vice-Consul at the Port of Ponce, was brilliant.[1] Nothing less could have been expected, given the well known taste and efficiency of the organizers, Messrs. Fitzgibbons, Eduardo Quesada, and Degetau.

Postponing the event for a week due to the dengue fever which had affected all families was wise, for the event would certainly not have been as brilliant when originally scheduled. The invitations, printed with gold letters on elegant paper, symbolized the dignity of the occasion and anticipated its splendor. In truth, the guests were both numerous and patrician. The fair sex was affable, accommodating, and elegant as always, seeming to communicate silently to Mr. Gottschalk: "We are the captivating flower of Ponce society; intoxicated by the stirring enchantment with which you have enraptured our souls, we come to you full of emotion in order to delight you with the magic of our perfumed presence." The guests of honor arrived just as the orchestra began to sound its first chords; upon their entrance all attention was focused on them, the assembled guests avidly projecting the closest friendship and admiration for those who had so delighted them at the theater.

The balcony of Mr. Lhose's house was handsomely decorated. Lamps placed among the foliage of green and fragrant branches and the garlands of flowers provided an exotic and elegant touch, as did two allegorical banners bearing such inscriptions as *Sitio de Zaragoza, Recuerdos de Puerto Rico, Norma, Casta diva,* and *La calesera.*[2]

Following Mr. Gottschalk and Miss Patti's entrance, dancing began which lasted with the greatest animation and in perfect order until 1:00 A.M. At this time the guests moved toward the neighboring house of Mr. Degetau, where a dinner had been prepared. The balcony of this house, also illuminated, produced a good effect, but what really aroused the admiration of all were the elegance and splendor with which the tables had been decorated, demonstrating to all the organizers' taste and intelligence. They had omitted nothing in honoring an event rooted in enthusiasm and in the purest and most cordial affection toward the artists, who by their merits and their cordiality had evoked these sentiments.

Among the infinite variety of rich and exquisite edibles towered a great cake in the shape of a mountain with a rocky path which spiraled toward the pinnacle, where Fame with her eternal trumpet proclaimed the name of Gottschalk. All of the ladies were seated, and six or seven gentlemen as well. Mr. Gottschalk, one of the guests of honor, showed himself to be as kind and as gallant as he is skilled by refusing to be seated, instead lavishing his attention on the assembled ladies, whose charm had captivated him.

As soon as the ladies had abandoned their posts and the gentlemen had to some degree placated their appetites, the merriment and the toasts commenced. Mr. Gottschalk's health, his glory, and his affability were toasted innumerable times and with deep and general emotion. In his turn Mr. Gottschalk thanked his hosts and offered a final toast, which went more or less as follows: "In attempting to reciprocate the expressions of affection which you have just rendered me, I first thought of addressing you in English or French, the two languages with which I am most familiar, but I have decided to do this in Spanish so that all might understand me and being sure that my linguistic errors will find your forbearance, because my words emanate from my heart. I conceive the artist in two ways: as an artist and as a man. The applause rendered to the artist flatters his vanity, but the reception proffered to the man gladdens his heart. Ponce, more than any other place, has paid me this double honor. My memories of Ponce will always be most pleasurable to me."

The emotion with which he pronounced this short address, whose exact words we are sorry not to be able to recall, endeared him even more to everyone, for we saw in his words not only the great artist but also the cultured gentleman, the philosopher who understands the heart. Then he proposed a toast to the organizers to whose diligence was owed the brilliance and the great success of the occasion. This much deserved toast was enthusiastically seconded, but among the crowd a voice was heard from the heart of one full of emotion: "And to the health of the one who could inspire in them such enthusiasm and such diligence!" After dinner everyone returned to the ballroom, and the dancing continued until four o'clock in the morning. During the party, all conversations dealt with Gottschalk's marvelous talent and with his accomplishments as an eminent composer, as a celebrated pianist, and as a highly educated and cultured person.

In conclusion, Mr. Gottschalk must understand by this and other testimonies which he has received that Ponce has simply but eloquently expressed its admiration for his artistic merits and its purest and most

cordial affection toward his simplicity, his frankness of character, and
his appealing charm, whose irresistible force is felt and obeyed but never
explained or understood.

Saint John's Day Mass in the Cathedral

Federico Asenjo y Arteaga, *Las Fiestas de San Juan: reseña histórica de
lo que han sido y de lo que son y relación verídica de las que se
celebraron en este año de 1868* (Puerto-Rico: Imprenta del Comercio,
1868), 154-61.[3]

The municipal government . . . paid for decorating the cathedral altar
of St. John the Baptist with lights and flowers. The entire cathedral orchestra played during the decennial and was augmented for the mass to
almost fifty performers, among whom were to be seen almost all of our
principal musicians plus a chorus of twelve voices.

The reader will allow me a moment to describe the music of the
mass. As I have previously had occasion to express, art enjoys the rare
ability to move the soul's most delicate fibers. For this reason it is natural that religion should employ that music which with its brilliant harmonies carries us enthusiastically and rapidly to the celestial heights in
which we faithfully contemplate the choruses of wingèd angels and cher-
ubim prostrate in obeisance before the All High; or that music whose
tender melodies lead us sweetly and mysteriously to the most hidden
depths of our own souls so that we might with its help pour out the re-
storing tears of repentance.

The mass performed for the second time in these Saint John's Day
festivities is the work of my friend, chapelmaster Felipe Gutiérrez, who
composed it in 1861 and dedicated it to the then and present bishop of
this diocese, the Most Excellent and Most Illustrious Dr. don Fr. Benig-
no Carrión de Málaga.[4]

Maestro Gutiérrez is very well known throughout Puerto Rico and
even abroad, but this fact does not excuse me from the pleasurable duty
of proffering him recognition and proclaiming him a distinguished Son
of Art. Rich in sentiment, fertile in conception, and profound master of
the secrets of harmony, Gutiérrez' works shine with all of the richness of
an imagination secure and glowing in its flight.

This St. John's Day Mass is without a doubt one of his finest compositions, and for this reason, as the motive for its composition was the
same as my motive for writing the present book, I believe it appropriate

to describe the work carefully. I hope that my friend Gutiérrez, as previously did my friend Oller[5] and in recognition of my honest intentions, will forgive the expressions of a layman in the arts who dares to emit not a critical judgment but only an opinion which although founded in good sense and in a definite fondness for all of the Fine Arts, is not supported by the solid knowledge which would be necessary to avoid frequent error.

The *Kyries* of the Gutiérrez mass are based on a hymn which we hear intoned in plainchant in the church, and for this reason possess that solemnity, that loftiness, that purity which distinguish religious hymns that do not age in spite of their years and centuries of existence, for on the contrary they are always heard with the same pleasure that accompanies a first hearing, as if they were new.

The *Gloria* is brilliant, but one wishes only that the first measures of the opening *andante* might be suppressed. In this part a certain lassitude is evident, a lassitude which does not concord with the liveliness of the rest of the composition. The work could begin without any problem with the following *allegro* itself. This melody, like the others which continue as far as the *Quoniam*, displays the composer's fecundity and good taste, for here, original melodies of the most exquisite sentiment abound. The tenor aria of the *Quoniam* suffers from a want of originality, but perhaps conscious of this lapse the composer has very successfully adorned it with a rich variation in the first violin. Here the composer demonstrates his cleverness as well as his perfect knowledge of orchestration and of the charm and interest which he can draw from each of his instruments.

The *Gloria* ends with a *moderato maestoso* of sweet and expressive song, in which is revealed the soul of the composer as it manifests his pure and modest tastes. There is in this music a most tender echo which awakens in the hearts of those who know the composer the memory of his great virtues as well as the simplicity which characterizes all of his actions. My friend Gutiérrez, who so assiduously studies the great musical masters, knows perfectly well that it is this simplicity which so pleases in the religious works of Miné[6] and in the paintings of Velázquez; he is thus well aware of the effect of the noble quality of simplicity.

The piece ends in a *presto* finale for the *In gloria Dei patris, Amen*, conceived in the fugal style so appropriate for church music. Here Gutiérrez demonstrates his solid and extensive knowledge as a composer, applying his rich imagination in the *motives* as well as in the *exposition* and the *episodes*, whose variety and whose good taste brilliantly close this worthy composition.

The *Credo* is of a class of music very superior to the *Gloria*, for in my humble opinion the latter destroys the unity of merit which should mark the entire mass. But the composer was probably carried away by the abundance of sentiments which dominate the *Gloria*, so different from each other and together so grand. The *Credo*, which contains the principal mysteries of our Holy Faith, could do nothing less than deeply move the composer's sensitive soul; for this reason the work is rich in effective contrasts and varied harmonies, all of which in my opinion raise it to the highest level of classical music. Above all, the *Incarnatus* section shines forth; full of majesty and solidity, it produces in the hearer the profound reverence which these elevated mysteries require.

The *allegro* of the *Resurrexit* perfectly echoes the rejoicing of the Church and of the faithful for the resurrection of Our Saviour, which in itself symbolizes the regeneration of the world. It is surprising for the novelty of the melody with which it concludes, for it seems as if the sounds distance themselves until they become imperceptible, followed immediately by another strain which as if at an equal distance, imitates the distant echo of a church organ. The first time this music is played by the brass instruments and the second time, closer to the place where the first group left off, it is repeated by the chorus and the entire orchestra. The effect both times is marvelous; this entire part of the mass is of a character so truly religious that on hearing it the soul becomes filled with that mystical essence which brings one close to God.

The music of the entire mass is rich with varied musical ornament and with instrumental solos which contribute to its embellishment. However, as a layman I dare to counsel my friend Gutiérrez that he not be so generous in either of these directions, and that he not extend the solos too much, as he did with the flügelhorn solo which precedes the *Benedictus*, for this practice only serves to distract the faithful from the true purpose which drew them to the temple, especially when solos are played by a skilled *maestro,* as on this occasion; these resources do not require the rich imagination of a Felipe Gutiérrez.

An Italian Opera Company

R.S., "Revista y crítica teatral," *Boletín Mercantil* (San Juan), 22 April 1877: 3.

On Saturday evening April 21, the opera company presented *Maria di Rohan,* by the immortal Donizetti, as the second opera in the subscription series.[7]

The theater was absolutely full, with the boxes occupied by members of the fair sex wearing luxurious dresses and precious jewelry of exquisite taste. These nymphs, of radiant beauty and gracious figure, were the great fascination of the opposite sex, who observed these charmers with languid glances. The opera began at 8:15. The scenery and other physical aspects were of the usual quality throughout the work, considering the little equipment and the few resources with which the theater is expected to present works of such brilliance.

The first act began with a well prepared introductory chorus, followed by a soprano aria sung by Miss D'Aponte. She nicely accentuated the *andante*, and expressed the *allegro* with energy and vigor; however, in the *fermata* or final cadenza we noted difficulty in passages of agility as well as the lack of force and roundness in the lower octave of her voice, which is customarily weak and therefore cannot produce the desired effect. It is a pity that Miss D'Aponte's sweet voice, of silvery and melodious timbre, does not possess equal strength throughout its range. The baritone *romanza* from *María de Radilla*,[8] which Mr. Petrilli sang instead of the one which Donizetti had composed, was masterfully presented, with correct technique in the spun-out notes and clear expression in every phrase. Mr. Petrilli's presentation gave us to understand that during the rest of the performance we would experience enthusiasm and complete satisfaction.

The orchestra: good, for which we congratulate Maestro Rosario Aruti. We hope that *Maria di Rohan* might be repeated one or more times so that persons who could not attend this first presentation might experience our same pleasure by attending a performance of an opera which was found so agreeable to all and which Puerto Rico will not soon forget.

Last Sunday evening we had the pleasure of attending the second performance of the opera *Traviata*. The attendance was truly sparse, but that should not surprise us as the work is very well known and as it so little pleased the general public on the evening of its first performance. In the first place, *Traviata*, whose plot is tasteless and immoral as everyone knows, lacks dramatic scenes but instead possesses trifling and disordered arias; it is perhaps for this reason that Mr. Petrilli did not please us in the role of Germont.

In the men's chorus the basses were good but the tenors weak. The orchestra played the fourth-act *soli* of violins well, but to produce the desired effect an orchestra needs more strings. In the absence of larger

string sections, even with excellent musicians there is not enough
strength of bowing among them to produce a healthy and indeed necessary effect. Opera needs a bigger orchestra, and especially in the strings.

Maestro Aruti, couldn't you enlarge the orchestra by two more first
violins and an additional double bass? We hope that the talented director
will be able to please us. We also wish that the cuts and other changes
which are made in the works might be announced on the posters.

In summary, having seen and heard *Traviata* and *Maria di Rohan* we
believe the company to be a good one, and we expect to enjoy many more
pleasant experiences. Therefore we recommend that music lovers take
advantage of the occasion to attend the theater every evening and enjoy
the beauty which by their very nature envelops each of the works announced for the first subscription series.

A Competition: The Ponce Exposition

José Ramón Abad, *Puerto Rico en la Feria-Exposición de Ponce en
1882. Memoria redactada de orden de la junta directiva de la misma*
(Ponce: Tipo. El Comercio, 1885), 82-84.[9]

In their considered and well warranted findings, the gentlemen of the
musical competition jury demonstrated profound knowledge of the sub-
lime and equally difficult art of music. Despite the severity with which
they had to apply the fundamental laws of harmony and counterpoint,
which must never be infringed upon with impunity; those of melody,
which show talent the path of the heart while endowing style with elegance and ideas with charm; those of unity, which adjoin the inspiration
of genius with the laws of art; those of artistic propriety, which by con-
cealing the difficulties of the craft displays the beauty of the design: despite this necessary rigor the jury had the satisfaction of certifying that
most of the submitted works honor their creators, while almost all of
them reveal gifts of ingenuity and talent which, carefully cultivated,
might reach a high level of artistic perfection.

Twenty-six compositions were submitted to the competition; seven of
these were orchestral works, another seven were for piano and twelve for
voice and piano. As the jury had to limit itself to the number of awards
available while honoring the relative merits of almost all of the works
submitted, it recognized the most outstanding compositions as follows:
gold medal and first class honorable mention to the sinfonía[10] *La Lira*,
which surpasses all others because the unity of its design, the beauty of

its style and its form, its meticulousness (except for minor blemishes), the clarity and good taste of its harmony, as well as its excellent orchestration, are united to the elegance of its themes and the mastery of its development.

As for works for voice and piano, the jury awarded the first prize, offered by the Board of Directors of the Fair, to the *romanza* "Alla Luna," and the prize offered by the Board of Directors of the Ponce Casino to the song "Lui."

The jury awarded the prize for the best composition for piano to the *Polonesa de Concierto*, with which no other entry could dispute the honor, for it unites such qualities that it might be judged a perfect work.

These awards having been determined, the jury decided that the second prize offered by the Board of Directors should be awarded to the *Obertura de Concierto*, whose musical discourse begins well and arrives at its conclusion without the interest of its phrases ever flagging.

Such was the decision of the jury for the awarding of prizes for written compositions, although it also recommended the piece entitled "Loarina," which among its beautiful passages manifests a tendency to raise itself to the level of great difficulties in musical composition; it also recommended the charming work for voice and piano entitled "Adiós," which was presented at the last minute and therefore could not be heard during the concert. The jury recommended special awards of equal rank for the two compositions.

Another hearing at the theater was required for the judging of the prizes offered by the Board of Directors for the conductors and the members of the orchestras which would play two works, one from the respective orchestra's own repertory and one to be played at sight, the latter to be assigned by the jury. On this occasion the winning compositions were also performed; the envelopes containing the composers' names were opened and the winners solemnly proclaimed. Preceded by just renown appeared the Sociedad de Conciertos orchestra from San Juan, conducted by don Fermín Toledo;[11] accepting the challenge, although without hope of winning such an unequal competition (as its director had previously asserted) was the orchestra of our own theater.[12]

A drawing determined the order in which the orchestras would perform, and the first turn fell to the Ponce orchestra, directed by don Juan Morel Campos. The orchestra played the grand march *Redención* by maestro Tavárez,[13] and the Sociedad de Conciertos orchestra played the sinfonía *Paragraphe*,[14] by maestro Suppé. In the same order the two orchestras played the *Obertura de Concierto* at sight without a single error; it was eloquently clear, however, that the Sociedad de Conciertos orchestra held a great advantage over its rival in the organization and discipline of its large membership.

The jury awarded the gold medal with first class honorable mention to the conductor of the latter orchestra, and the silver medal and second class honorable mention to each of its members. The president of the jury, don Virgilio Biaggi, presented Mr. Toledo with a score of the opera *Nibelungen* by maestro Wagner, arranged for piano; the jury, taking into account the efforts taken by maestro Juan Morel Campos in honorably sustaining the noble battle which he had undertaken with an almost improvised orchestra, recommended to the Board of Directors that he be honored in whatever way might be deemed appropriate.[15]

Mrs. Spencer de Graham[16] then sang the *romanza* "Alla Luna" and the song "Lui" with great skill and precision. The envelopes containing the names of the winning composers were opened; the first is by don José Agulló y Prats and the second by don Fermín Toledo, on a text by don A. Biaggi.

The *Obertura de Concierto*, also awarded a prize, was revealed to be by don Casimiro Duchesne. The *Polonesa de Concierto,* which was awarded a silver medal and first class honorable mention, was composed by don Fermín Toledo, and the public had the great pleasure of hearing it performed on the piano by maestro Manuel Tavárez. The theater orchestra then played the sinfonía *La Lira*, which had won the first prize, and the outstanding young maestro Juan Morel Campos was revealed as its composer.

Several members of the jury brought to the attention of the Board of Directors the great merits of Maestro Tavárez' grand march *Redención*, which, as arranged for piano, possesses the attributes of a perfect work, original and inspired. Its author had not wished to enter it in the competition as he had agreed to serve as a member of the jury. The Board, considering the merits of the work and the delicacy with which its composer had conducted himself, decreed that he be awarded a gold medal and first-class honorable mention.

The Philharmonic Society

Alejandro Tapia y Rivera, *Mis memorias o Puerto Rico como lo encontré y como lo dejo* [1880] (New York: De Laisne & Rossboro, Inc., [1928]), 105-106.[17]

In 1846 I abstained from calling on Salomé because I didn't receive any encouragement from her mother, although I longed to see her and talk to her. With this in mind and with the collaboration of some friends and their relatives, I conceived the idea of giving a dance across the street from the Cathedral. We personally invited the leading figures of San Juan, and the dance was a brilliant success.[18]

I spoke with Salomé at my pleasure at the dance, as she had come without her mother. Actually, her mother liked me very much but was opposed to my courting her daughter and rightly so, for I had no position and was very young, in fact younger than Salomé herself.

We were very pleased with the success of the dance, and I decided to repeat it. We persuaded some of the more serious, more mature, and more influential members of the *jeunesse dorée* to help us. They apparently had some similar idea themselves, but they liked our project and joined their efforts to ours. From this beginning developed a society which organized not only dances, but social entertainments and concerts as well.

This was the origin of the Philharmonic Society, which was to contribute to the island's cultural life in these and other ways.[19] In truth my friends and I didn't aspire so highly, but the members of the other group (Cabrera, Iriarte, Carcerán, Elzaburu, and others) gave the project form and polish. Our own contribution was mainly in general helpfulness and youthful enthusiasm; without the others the society would not have survived beyond a dance or two, living only as long as the lovesickness of some of the members. As for me, my zeal was entirely rooted in my desire to see and talk to Salomé; if my exertions in founding the Philharmonic Society were great, they were due to the one who inspired in me the whole enterprise. From what modest beginnings much greater things can grow! No one else in my group was so devoted to the project, but my ardent participation and the great enthusiasm which I brought to the task are explained by youth's apparent frivolity.

The Philharmonic Society, as it was called, began its activities in December 1846, if I remember correctly, with elegant and fashionable events favored by San Juan's highest society. Concerts, social entertainments, dances: all brilliant and lively. In addition to the increasing number of ladies and gentlemen who sang and played musical instruments, there was a mixed chorus made up of the most *comme il faut* youth of the time. There was a music school and the organization of an amateur orchestra was undertaken, which also included some salaried professionals.[20]

A stage was built in the Society's main hall, and was inaugurated on the first of January, 1849. This stage was used for concerts and poetry recitals, and here was also launched an amateur drama group formed by members of the Society.

The San Juan Municipal Theater

Manuel Fernández Juncos, "El Teatro," in his *Galería Puerto-Riqueña: Costumbres y Tradiciones* (San Juan: Biblioteca de "El Buscapié," 1883), 115-20.[21]

Let us now consider that ancient structure down at the end of the city, bounded on the north by Plaza Santiago, on the south by an abandoned artillery post now used as a bath house and for other disreputable purposes, on the east by the Puerta de Tierra wall and on the west by O'Donnell Street, formerly known as Star Alley.[22]

This is an edifice of strange aspect and unusual construction, which bears the characteristic stamp of the period in which it was built. The extreme solidity of its walls, more than two meters thick; the system of inclined planes instead of steps found in the side aisles; the narrow arches of its doors, the dissimilar corridors, the underground passages and other means of more or less strategic communication, and the towers which crown the back part of the building: all provide a pronounced military aspect, while the portico's symmetrical arches, the design of the windows and grillwork, the gabled roof, and the façade's triangular finial attract the attention of the curious traveler, who would probably write something like the following in his notebook:

"Puerto-Rico—Theater. Edifice of curious and ancient design, halfway between fort and convent, which offers to the observer the eccentric spectacle of a great cage with suggestions of a powder magazine."

Such, dear readers, is the place which we have dedicated to the cult of Melpomene and Thalia and which from time to time also serves for dances, meetings, gymnastic exercises, magic shows, and displays of fleas, rats, dogs, and other animals equally wise but of differing numbers of feet.

But while it is true that the exterior provides no indication of the purpose to which such a building might be devoted, it would be enough to peep through one of its doors to suspect that it is a theater, simply by reading one of the notices displayed within, which reads as follows: "We beg you not to smoke or spit on the stage."

One later discovers other details which leave no doubt in this matter, such as the narrow rows of seats, some rather rickety to be sure and almost always covered with dust and rust, implacable enemies of white clothing; the strange design of the *house*[23] and the main *boxes*, set into the walls or rather attached to them like swallows' nests; the humble and economical *orchestra seats*; the uncomfortable *side boxes* and the lofty *balcony*. All of these areas are efficiently distributed under a ceiling more or less flat, studded with nails and stars and decorated with gilded figures representing a bull, a goat, a scorpion, a crab, a pair of fishes, and other significant animals.

Then one observes the curtain, alias the *rag*, as theater chroniclers and writers have been given to calling it; in truth, this epithet might quite justly be applied to the theater's decor as well.

Having arrived at the curtain, it would be good for my readers to accompany me backstage so that we might quickly examine the sets, the properties, the machinery, the furniture, and everything that in theater language is referred to as *the soul of the theater*; in this way we can learn what kind of soul the theater of this capital city has.

That curtain of indefinable color which extends from the stage up into the *flies* is the *cyclorama*, representing the horizon; the dark strip which you see at the top is . . . the sea! Pay no attention to the grim and stormy appearance of the horizon itself; this could be its habitual appearance or the result of some accident. It might appear to us as a terrible and threatening cloud, unless it were simply a water stain, or a badly made seam, or a miserable repair job.

The next one is a *great forest drop*. Consider, please, how great the forest is if the spectator can distinguish in it only holes, scrawls, and grease spots. And that one is a *garden drop* which might still serve as such, if one were to place before it a fence, some fountains and statues, several natural plants and shrubs and a sign explaining what it all represents. Following it is a piece which in other times represented the Plaza of the Martyrs but which now represents only its own martyrdom, caused by time's implacable hand.

In front of this *garden* or *plaza* is sometimes hung an ancient *Gothic hall*, so designated not so much for the design of its columns as for the great number of holes which adorn it. The next one, delapidated and worthless, was at a time of greater fortune and prosperity a *princely salon*. Now, lord love us, it suggests neither princeliness nor prosperity, and resembles more a house of tatters than a hall worthy of a sovereign.

That other one is a *convent drop*, which also serves as a tavern, a castle, a rustic house, a graveyard, the gates of Bethlehem, a madhouse, and other such scenes. Next is a drop whose original purpose is unknown, but it is used today to represent a storm, a distant forest, a dark street, etc. White strips of canvas or paper are attached to it when necessary; it then represents the sea, with waves.

There are also a *small salon*, two *closed rooms*, and a *forest*; a *large plaza* is in such lamentable state that it reminds us of the destruction of Troy or the ruinous San Felipe hurricane. The furniture and minor properties are fully worthy of the major pieces just described; their inventory comprises the following items: The face of a tower with high grillwork. A screen in the form of a wall, for *La conquista de Lorca* and the last act of *Guzmán el Bueno*. A long and narrow box in the shape of a stone bench, which can also serve as *the tomb of doña Inés*. A half-dozen imitation cork and apple trees. Four pieces which can represent the edge of a forest. The door of a miserable room, which can also serve as a garden gate or the grilled door of a monastery. Turned differently it becomes a cooking grate or an auto-da-fe, a platform for the torture of blessed souls. A couple of *painted pine* tables. Four mirror frames with mirrors of warped cardboard. Two Gothic chairs of *pitch pine*. A half dozen benches. Four military tents. A platform. A sedan chair resembling a stretcher. And a triumphal chariot made of tin and cardboard.

And more: Two canvas statues in bad condition; two large urns of the same material; four inscribed gravestones; two crosses; a column and a stuffed figure representing the god Mercury with his canvas platform and his symbolic staff, larger than a drum major's baton.

Here you have San Juan's theater in body and soul. For some years the municipal government has planned a project for the renovation of the theater, and if such a project should ever reach completion I have wished to provide my readers with this brief sketch, if only to preserve the memory of the old theater and its effects, which have served for more than forty years.

In the name of Heaven and the Municipal Government, before the year 1877 is out may this sketch have passed to the realm of memory![24]

Music and Advertising in
Nineteenth-Century San Juan

Edgardo Díaz Díaz, "Música para anunciar en la sociedad sanjuanera del siglo XIX," *Revista Musical Puertorriqueña*, no. 1 (January-June 1987): 6-12.

References in the nineteenth-century Puerto Rican press provide information dealing with the use of music in advertising. It is commonly believed that such practices came into use only in the present century, resulting from the application of modern techniques of influencing human behavior. The present study indicates that certain advertising techniques, motivated by the need to survive in business in nineteenth century Puerto Rico, anticipated the formulation of modern marketing theories. It also sheds light on some specific advertising practices, introduced in Puerto Rico mainly by Cuban and peninsular Spanish manufacturers.

The use of martial flourishes to call attention to official edicts was the first association of sounds with public announcements to be noted in Puerto Rico. The first known mention dates from 1568, when to the sound of drum rolls performed by an official drummer, San Juan authorities announced "in the streets and crossroads" a judgment brought against a couple living in concubinage.[25]

Through the use of such devices residents were frequently informed of events occurring in the distant capital of the Spanish monarchy. Such announcements were frequently preceded by the sound of bells, cannon, or drums, symbolizing the powerful source of the announcements themselves: church, garrison, or civil authority. Colonial subjects were in this way called upon to share the joys and sorrows of their distant masters. The following rhymed text, read in public, exemplifies the mourning of the Spanish government upon the announcement of the death of King Felipe V in 1746:

Las campañas tañidas
resuenan repetidas,
estemplados tambores
publican sus dolores
y el bronce con bramidos
dava sus alaridos:
a todos causa espanto
con su violento llanto;
veinte y cuatro horas llora
bostezando el cuadrante de la hora.[26]

Funeral observances for Felipe V had barely ended when the authorities published an edict "to the sound of drums and bugles," ordering the cessation of mourning and calling upon residents to manifest their joy at the confirmation of Fernando VI as absolute Spanish monarch.[27]

Due to the great distance between Spain and Puerto Rico and also due to the frustrating indifference which Spain exhibited toward the legitimate aspirations of established island settlers, relations between "Spaniards from Spain" and native-born Puerto Ricans were not always cordial. Nevertheless, the atmosphere of noisy celebration which was associated with the official recognition of occurrences in distant Spain aided in reinforcing the image and the political presence of the monarchy. Until the early nineteenth century, reports of royal festivities observed in Puerto Rico and throughout the Spanish world confirm the use of bugles and drums to announce the public reading of all kinds of announcements.

Pealing bells and roaring cannon remained effective symbols and part of island life until the spirit of royally decreed festivities accompanied the decline of the monarchy's importance in the 1870s. When the Spanish military felt the negative effects of the high cost of the Cuban war and other military campaigns, in addition to the general decline of Spanish morale and other factors, the gradual disappearance of roaring cannon and muffled drums began.

The introduction of the printing press and the establishment of the newspaper *La Gaceta* as the organ of the government in Puerto Rico occurred around 1806, and the publication of edicts and other official announcements came to occupy the paper's first pages. This brought about an important shift in the medium of transmission: transferred from the earlier mode of orally transmitted public messages as street cries (*pregones*), official announcements were now fixed in print. As the public announcement lost its importance as a means of official communication, then, it became associated with street cries in the popular tradition of commercial use. As a result, several earlier techniques, such as some intonational and rhythmic styles, were embraced by vendors from marginalized sectors of society. They were then employed in street cries, bringing new musical and esthetic dimensions to the tradition of public divulgation.

Newspaper references to the commercial street cry, i.e., a musical cry or shout conceived to advertise a specific product, sometimes displayed a contemptuous tone and at other times praised the effort, depending basically on the vendor's social class or on the style of his text and tune. According to a later report, in June 1822 the *Diario Liberal y de Variedades* (San Juan) published a communication from "An ignorant person but one interested in this matter" which complained of the bedlam caused by charcoal and vegetable vendors at the Plaza de la

Constitución (now Plaza de Armas).[28] No further information is available regarding this particular complaint, but it is known from other sources that the Plaza de la Constitución was the site of an open produce market,[29] and we are led to believe that vendors would use their voices in advertising their merchandise.

Mainly due to the lack of newspaper sources for long periods of the nineteenth century, we find no mention of ambulant vendors until the following observation, dating from the end of 1877:

> Touts constantly run about the city, chanting insistently on all the notes of the scale: '¡Pasteles calientes!, ¡Maní tostado!, ¡Espada y galletitas!, ¡Rosquitas y pan de huevo!, ¡Sopa borracha!, ¡Dulce fino!, etc., etc.'[30]

It is possible to attribute the rise of the ambulant merchant in those years to a congestion of vendors in the plazas and their subsequent banishment to the streets. On the other hand it may have been at least partly due to an influx of freed slaves after the abolition of slavery in 1873: newcomers to the city who sought their livelihood on street corners and in alleyways.

References in the press to ambulant vendors become more frequent in the last third of the century, and they mainly express irritation at the screeching and the commotion, in much the same way that blacks' *bomba* dancing was described. In the context of the social attitudes of the time, reading between the lines reveals more than the simple expression of opinions. We know, for example, that a decree of 1878 temporarily prohibited the cries and shouts of ambulant vendors, and from the same source we also know something of the techniques which vendors employed. For example, the insistent nature of the shouting was described as peculiar, outlandish, unexpected. Secondly, vendors explored a repertory of effects, seeking the most effective formula by singing or chanting "on all the notes."[31] In addition to the foods mentioned above, street vendors also offered other products of artisan manufacture. Vocal style displayed considerable embellishment[32] in musically describing the merchandise.[33]

Music for advertising was not limited to vocal expression. Candy peddlers were described in 1880 as using bells and *matracas* (wooden rattles),[34] while in 1889 ice was sold to the accompaniment of trumpet music played by boys.[35]

Tolerance of San Juan's street vendors may have increased during the last years of the century, for newspapers carried few complaints against *pregones* and other clangorous forms of advertising. Meanwhile, the presence of street vendors in such places as Jayuya[36] and Bayamón[37] indicates the spread to towns and villages of this popular method of advertising as business conducted by small vendors increased outside San Juan. Beginning at midcentury the commercial structure of such centers as San Juan and Ponce displayed increasing complexity. Consumers, in addition to buying necessary items, now found a great number of other products both fashionable and available. Changes were occurring in urban life; a new kind of consumer came into being with new attitudes toward commerce and advertising, rejecting the strident imposition of merchandise on the listener's consciousness.

It became necessary for merchants to refine their methods of presenting and describing types of merchandise, with the merchandise now preferably located at fixed locations and awaiting the approach of customers. Merchants had to develop innovative advertising techniques adapted to the latest styles and with the explicit purpose of announcing, identifying and describing, not immediately selling, a product. The humble ambulant vendor, the *pregonero*, could not meet these demands. For this reason he had to take to the streets to display his merchandise, as he had no shop in which to await the arrival of customers. Moreover, he had to sell quickly due to the speed with which his merchandise, mainly produce, deteriorated.

Programs of outdoor concerts offered by the regimental bands stationed in Puerto Rico document the extent to which commercial houses benefited from advertising through music. During a concert in Ponce in January 1857 the Cádiz Regiment Band played a *paso doble* entitled "El Fénix," the name of a Ponce newspaper.[38] Other titles allusive to business houses appeared in band concert programs, especially in the last decades of the century, and were effective as advertising. However, a considerable number of them were not specifically conceived as advertising but rather represented a friendly gesture on the part of the composer.

Friendly gestures might be reflected in such titles as "La Elegancia Puertorriqueña," a *danza* by H. Aruti and C. Padilla dedicated to the store which bore that name;[39] "La Correspondencia de Puerto Rico," a *danza* by Bartolomé Díaz and dedicated to the newspaper of the same name;[40] "París Bazar," a mazurka dedicated by composer Braulio Dueño to Pedro Giusti, owner of the París Bazar store;[41] and "La Pilarica," a *danza* dedicated to the owners of that store by composer Casimiro Duchesne.[42]

These titles refer not to specific products but to business establishments. On the other hand, advertising a specific product or a brand name through music was indeed a commercial arrangement for the composer, unlike the cases cited above. As for the cost of advertising with music, engaging even a semi-professional ensemble could cost a considerable sum. Once again we find the street vendor at a disadvantage, for only businesses with a high volume of production and sales could afford to advertise their products with more demanding or more sophisticated music.

This privileged position was in fact occupied mainly by such imported merchandise as liquor and tobacco products. The earliest evidences of such advertising date from 1885, in an observation published in a San Juan newspaper: "Night before last, a group of musicians roamed through the streets extolling the virtues of Estanillo cigarettes. An ingenious way to advertise!"[43]

The practice of advertising with orchestras or bands, as described in the press, was perhaps introduced by Cuban or peninsular Spanish entrepreneurs. The only reference which has appeared to a "jingle" commissioned by a native industrialist during the nineteenth century is to a waltz entitled "Alcoholado Gatell," ordered from composer Juan Morel Campos. The piece was performed in San Juan by the band of the Madrid Regiment in 1887.[44]

In 1891 and 1892 the distillery of Rafael Romero, in Jerez de la Frontera, Spain, commissioned two *danzas* by Puerto Rican composers, to be played on the public plazas. One, "Ponche Militar" by Casimiro Duchesne, was performed in November 1891 in the Plaza de Armas, San Juan, by the Institute of Volunteers Band. Its allusive text was displayed on an illuminated balloon or globe.[45] The other advertising *danza* was "El Cognac Jerez," by Juan Morel Campos. Surviving is a reduction for piano, whose style and spirit mark the work as a characteristic Morel Campos festive *danza*. The only feature which distinguishes it from its many sisters is its text, part of which rhymes as follows: "Si agitan vuestras almas/ Anhelos de placer/ Pedid puertorriqueñas/ Pedid Cognac Jerez."[46] With its appeal to Puerto Rican ladies to consume a specific product, "Cognac Jerez" suggests a degree of sophistication which targeted potential consumers according to a specific sector of society: in this case, women. This technique of social differentiation is frequently encountered in today's advertising practices directed toward specific markets.

Another *danza* of Morel was commissioned by the house of Celorio and Mora of Havana, with a title referring to the "El Fígaro" brand of cigarettes. The Volunteers Band performed the piece with a chorus of 35 voices in February 1892, producing a "surprising effect."[47]

Retretas, evening band concerts presented in the open spaces of city and town plazas, were important events accessible to all social classes. In this sense they performed the functions served today by the radio and television transmission of both concert and popular music. Programs consisted of *danzas*, mazurkas, waltzes and other light pieces along with band arrangements of works from the European concert repertory.

The importance of the regimental bands to this musical activity illustrates the integration of military forces in island life right up to the end of the century; so integrated were the bands that commercial houses used them for advertising. The practice of musical advertising in San Juan band concerts culminated during the first six months of 1892. Of some 42 concerts performed in the Plaza de Armas during this period, 13 (approximately one third) offered "jingles" which advertised firms or products. After July, a significant decrease took place in the frequency of such performances, a decrease which continued until the Spanish American War in 1898 and the beginning of a new chapter in Puerto Rican social history.[48]

It seems clear that the associative advertising techniques practiced in Puerto Rico a century ago were essentially the same as some which have been in effect during the present century. An additional illustration of the advertising inventiveness of a century ago is in the association of a specific product with the name of some noted musical figure. The titles of favorite operas and zarzuelas also appeared in this connection, as did the names of renowned composers and performers.

For example, considerable newspaper space was devoted to advertising the qualities of "La Patti" cigarettes, named for the admired opera soprano Adelina Patti,[49] and to "El Fígaro" and "El Rey que Rabió" cigarettes, evoking the respective opera (*The Marriage of Figaro*) and zarzuela.[50] Products bearing titles allusive to musical works and musical celebrities received free publicity through performances of the works or by the celebrities themselves, in contexts supposedly free from commercial interest.

Similar to the endorsement of Scott's Emulsion by Dr. Ramón Emeterio Betances, who urged "martyrs of health" to buy that product, was the endorsement of musical instruments by the island's most admired performers. For example, pianist Ana Otero was contracted by the Chickering company to endorse and demonstrate its pianos.[51] Pedro Giusti, proprietor of the París Bazar house of musical instruments and miscellaneous effects in San Juan, used a letter from pianist Gonzalo Núñez, then in Cuba, to support his advertising for his line of Bernareggi & Estrella pianos.[52]

Conclusion

Practices in musical advertising, observed in San Juan beginning well over a century ago, resulted from a long and complex historical process. The need for economic survival, native creative ability, and the expansionist spirit of foreign commercial activity were forces in this development. The earlier practice of reciting government edicts to the accompaniment of musical instruments and the proclamation of formal official festivities with bells, cannon and drums were principal modes of official announcement. At the beginning of the nineteenth century, street vendors of marginalized communities adopted and enriched such forms as the *pregón*, no longer in use for official purposes, to create new styles of chanting for purposes of selling their merchandise. The rise of foreign-based commercial activity in Puerto Rico and the participation of the Spanish military bands, linked to the tastes and early marketing experience of the island population, also contributed to the development of indigenous modes of advertising through music.

Notes

1. Louis Moreau Gottschalk (1829-1869) was the first U.S. musician to attain recognition abroad. At the time of his second Caribbean tour (1857-1859) he was approaching the height of his powers as a pianist and composer. Adelina Patti (1843-1919), later to become one of the most famous of all opera singers, was at the time of this tour an extremely promising adolescent singer; her professional U.S. debut took place after her return from the Caribbean. The Gottschalk-Patti concerts in Puerto Rico established a landmark in the island's concert life.

2. Titles of works associated with the Gottschalk-Patti tour.

3. A modern reprint can be seen: San Juan: Editorial Borinquen, 1971.

4. Felipe Gutiérrez y Espinosa (1825-1899) was probably Puerto Rico's most versatile and most distinguished nineteenth-century composer. *Maestro de Capilla* (music director) of the San Juan Cathedral from 1858 until the post was eliminated with the suppression of direct governmental support of the Church under U.S. rule, Gutiérrez composed a great deal of church music, as well as secular music and the only nineteenth-century Puerto Rican opera preserved today: *Macías*. For studies of Gutiérrez' life and works see Gustavo Batista, "Felipe Gutiérrez y Espinosa y el ambiente musical en el San Juan de su época" (M.A. thesis, Centro de Estudios Avanzados de Puerto Rico y el Caribe [San

Juan], 1982) and *Catálogo temático de la música de Felipe Gutiérrez y Espinosa (1825-1899)*, Guillermo Menéndez Maysonet, comp. (San Juan: Comisión para la Celebración del V Centenario de la Evangelización en Puerto Rico de la Conferencia Episcopal Puertorriqueña, 1993).

5. Francisco Oller (1833-1917), noted painter, also active in San Juan as a skilled singer.

6. The reference may be to Jean-Baptiste Minne (1734-ca.1817), Netherlandish painter of portraits and religious scenes.

7. The 1877-1878 appearances in Puerto Rico of this company, headed by baritone Egisto Petrilli, were among the most successful of a long series of visits by European companies which began in 1835 and continued to the end of the century and beyond. The Petrilli company performed in San Juan, Ponce, Mayagüez, and Aguadilla, with a repertory of some twenty extremely popular operas including works by Rossini, Donizetti, Bellini, Verdi, Halevy, Gounod, Marchetti, and the brothers Ricci. See Emilio J. Pasarell, *Orígenes y desarrollo de la afición teatral en Puerto Rico* (San Juan, 1951-1967), repr. San Juan: Departamento de Instrucción Pública, 1969.

8. *Maria Padilla*, also by Donizetti.

9. A facsimile ed. can be seen: San Juan: Editorial Coquí, 1967. The Ponce fair has often been described, with its musical significance placed in context in such works as Fernando Callejo Ferrer, *Música y músicos portorriqueños* (1915); reprinted, Amaury Veray, ed. (San Juan: Editorial Coquí, 1971), 181-83 and Donald Thompson, "El ambiente musical en Puerto Rico en la década de 1880," *Cupey* (Río Piedras, P.R.) 6, no. 1-2 (1989): 120-39. Having observed the decline and final discontinuation of governmentally decreed fairs (San Juan: 1854, 1855, 1860, 1865, and 1871), the municipality of Ponce, with a great deal of enthusiastic support from private persons and specific groups, organized the great Ponce Fair and Exposition of July 1-16, 1882, an event which for decades provided an important landmark in music and many other fields of endeavor in Puerto Rico. Every day of the fair was filled with ceremonial activities, parades, and balls, and music was present in virtually all such events, drawing musicians and ensembles from all parts of the island. The present excerpt describes two particularly important events: a composition competition and an orchestral match which would long be remembered as an episode in a traditional rivalry between San Juan and Ponce.

10. Concert overture.

11. Toledo, a peninsular Spaniard, was active in San Juan as a teacher, organizer, and music store proprietor. In 1883 he moved his business to New York City, but with the outbreak of the Spanish American War in 1898 he returned to Europe.

12. La Perla Theater, opened in 1864 and destroyed by fire in 1918. The present La Perla Theater, constructed on the same site, was opened in 1941.

13. Manuel Gregorio Tavárez (1842-1883), Morel's teacher. For the date of Tavarez' birth as given here, see Donald Thompson, "El joven Tavárez: nuevos documentos y nuevas perspectivas," *Revista del Centro de Estudios Avanzados de Puerto Rico y el Caribe* no. 11 (1990): 64-74.

14. *Paragraph Drei.*

15. Morel was awarded a silver medal and second class honorable mention; the members of his orchestra were awarded second class honorable mention.

16. A very able and extremely active singer resident in Ponce and better known as Lizzie Graham.

17. Tapia's work has been reprinted (San Juan, 1946), with another reprint at Río Piedras: Editorial Edil, 1979. Prior to its publication in book form Tapia's *Memorias* had appeared, serialized, in *La Democracia* (San Juan), during 1927. Alejandro Tapia y Rivera (1826-1882) was one of Puerto Rico's foremost literary figures. Poet, playwright, novelist, and opera librettist, Tapia also contributed greatly to the knowledge of the history of Puerto Rico through the publication of his *Biblioteca histórica de Puerto Rico* (Mayagüez, 1854), a collection of important documents compiled in Spain by him and other young Puerto Ricans studying there.

18. This dance may have taken place on November 26, 1845. See Pasarell, *Orígenes*, 80, citing an unidentified number of the *Gaceta de Puerto Rico.*

19. This was the second Philharmonic Society to be formed in San Juan; the first was organized in 1823.

20. According to Pasarell, *Orígenes*, 81, citing the *Gaceta de Puerto Rico*, December 11, 1845, the first concert sponsored by the new organization took place on December 9, 1845. Tapia's memory may have deceived him by one year.

21. A more recent edition exists: Concha Meléndez, ed. (San Juan, Instituto de Cultura Puertorriqueña, 1958). The construction of the San Juan Municipal Theater began in 1824, and the building was used for official festivities in 1830. The first known use of the structure as a public theater took place in 1832, with concerts by the English singers William and Anna Pearman. The theater was named for playwright Alejandro Tapia y Rivera following an extensive restoration in 1937, and still serves as an important site of theatrical and musical activities. See Donald Thompson, "Notes on the Inauguration of the San Juan (Puerto Rico) Municipal Theater," *Latin American Music Review* 11, no. 1 (June 1990): 84-91. The theater's most recent renovation was completed in 1997.

22. Plaza Santiago was renamed Plaza Colón in 1892 in commemoration of the fourth centennial of Columbus' discovery of Puerto Rico on his second voyage. The Puerta de Tierra wall was razed in 1897, permitting the growth of San Juan eastward into the part of the city known as Puerta de Tierra.

23. This and many other words are italicized in the original, in order to humorously emphasize the perceived peculiarity of theatrical terminology.

24. Author's note: "This article was written before the remodeling of the building took place in 1879, as a result of which the interior was completely changed. With this remodeling, ably directed by the distinguished engineer Tulio

Larrinaga, the old structure has been so improved that today it might find a place among the principal second class Spanish theaters. In spite of the remodeling of the theater, we have considered it appropriate to reprint this article as a reminder of the condition of the San Juan theater until recent date."

25. *Boletín Histórico de Puerto Rico* 12, no. 1 (1925): 138-40. Except where indicated, notes are by the author.

26. (Ed.) Pealing bells resound and echo; muffled drums announce their grief and the roaring cannon emits its howl, its violent cry bringing dread to all. Twenty-four hours it mourns, marking each quarter-hour's passing. *Boletín Histórico*, 5 (1918): 157.

27. *Boletín Histórico*, 164.

28. La Correspondencia de Puerto Rico 5, no. 1820 (27 November 1895): 2.

29. *Diario Liberal y de Variedades* 3, no. 35 (4 June 1822): 139-40.

30. (Ed.) Hot meat pies, roasted peanuts, fine sweets and other delicacies. *El Buscapié* (San Juan) 1, no. 39 (23 December 1877): 1.

31. *Boletín Mercantil de Puerto Rico* 39, no. 118 (9 October 1878): 3.

32. *Boletín Mercantil* 40, no. 4 (9 January 1881): 3.

33. *Boletín Mercantil* 44, no. 100 (1 September 1882): 3.

34. *Boletín Mercantil* 41, no. 39 (2 April 1880): 3.

35. *El Magisterio de Puerto Rico* 1, no. 24 (16 June 1889): 5-6.

36. *El Diario de Puerto Rico* 2, no. 212 (2 February 1894): 3.

37. *La Correspondencia* 8, no. 2740 (11 June 1898): 1.

38. *El Fénix* 2, no. 82 (24 January 1857): 2-3.

39. *Boletín Mercantil* 51, no. 48 (24 April 1889): 3; 51, no. 49 (26 April 1889): 3.

40. *La Correspondencia* 2, no. 699 (18 November 1892): 2.

41. *El Diario* 2, no. 294 (26 April 1894): 3.

42. *La Correspondencia* 5, no. 1767 (5 October 1895): 3.

43. *Boletín Mercantil* 42, no. 54 (8 May 1885): 3. The use of music in advertising was later observed in other towns. The firm Cerecedo Brothers, Mayagüez, hired an orchestra to publicize the Portagás brand of cigarettes. See *La Correspondencia* 2, no. 398 (21 January 1892): 3. The Carolina Volunteers Band played pleasant *danzas* to advertise Las Delicias, a local restaurant. See *La Correspondencia* 2, no. 597 (8 August 1892): 2. When the governmental monopoly on matches came to an end in 1895, Vicente Montañez, a San Lorenzo merchant, engaged a characteristic country ensemble to wander the streets advertising the matches offered at his store at one centavo the box. See *La Correspondencia* 5, no. 1725 (24 August 1895): 3.

44. *Boletín Mercantil* 49, no. 29 (9 March 1887): 3.

45 *Boletín Mercantil* 53, no. 137 (20 November 1891): 3.

46. (Ed.) If a wish for pleasure excites you, Puerto Rican ladies, ask for Cognac Jerez. *Boletín Mercantil* 44, no. 145 (7 December 1892): 3.

47. *La Correspondencia* 2, no. 431 (23 February 1892): 2; *Boletín Mercantil* 59, no. 24 (24 February 1892): 3.

48. *La Correspondencia* 2, nos. 380, 408, 412, 416, 431, 450, 461, 468, 478, 522, 529, 537, and 551, all 1892.

49. *La Correspondencia* 5, no. 1777 (15 October 1895): 4.

50. *La Correspondencia* 5, no. 1652 (12 June 1895): 3.

51. *La Correspondencia* 2, no. 716 (5 December 1892): 2.

52. *La Correspondencia* 5, no. 1538 (18 February 1895): 2.

4

THE PUERTO RICAN *DANZA*

The *danza puertorriqueña*, originally a form of dance music closely related to the Spanish *contradanza*, has attracted a great deal of attention
in Puerto Rico ever since its first appearance almost a century and a half
ago. Writers have debated its origins and the phases of its development
while fathers of young ladies have questioned its propriety. The *danza*
has enlivened fashionable balls and public dance halls alike; it has also
formed a basis for concert music and a vehicle for love songs. It has been
seen by some as the perfect musical reflection of the island's planter aris-
tocracy, but others hear in it the dissenting voice of a plebeian artisan
class. On the other hand, some observers have seen the *danza* as symbolic of Puerto Rican society and Puerto Rican culture in general. More
recently, others have asked "Just which society and whose culture are we
talking about, anyway?" The *danza* has experienced decades of neglect
and brief periods of enthusiastic revival, while the exploration of its
technical aspects has inspired masters' theses and doctoral dissertations.
Perhaps the best evidence of Puerto Rico's undying regard for this hardy
nineteenth-century dance form is the fact that a beloved *danza*, "La
borinqueña," was chosen as the official anthem of the Commonwealth of
Puerto Rico in 1952.

The *Danza* Controversy:
An Early Skirmish

(1) Ponce, August 24, 1853
To the Editor, *El Ponceño*[1]

Endowed only with my status as a woman (a woman whose most
delicate sensibilities have been wounded and one eager to defend the

prerogatives of her sex), I respectfully address you in the hope of gaining the protection which since its founding *El Ponceño* has proffered to our cause—the cause of the weaker sex—and beg you to lend your attention to my just complaint by granting a little space in your paper to the following observations, which in the name of my friends I address to all of the lost and misguided young gentlemen of Ponce who dare to frequent dances organized by persons other than ourselves.

As I see it, society can be compared to the steam engine on father's plantation, whose various parts, each functioning separately, are never hindered in their respective motions except for the contact and the friction necessary to attain the general result. On the contrary, they twirl and pivot continuously, given the specific condition that each part must remain in the station determined by the machine's designer. Thus the parts never collide with one another, which would produce a violent disturbance in the regularity of the machine's functioning. Please forgive me the peculiarity of this comparison, but everyone finds his analogies in the things and the impressions which most strike his imagination or which are most agreeable to his ideas. For my part I must confess that few things have pleased me more than the sight of the steam engine on father's plantation, particularly the reciprocating motion of that great piston, at once so smooth and so irresistible.

Well, then; I was saying that in my view and just as in the case of father's machine, each rank and class of the society in which we live, each circle of our social sphere, moves within determined limits beyond which the individual should not and indeed cannot venture without risking a clash with unknown bodies. These foreign bodies, as they do not move within the same orbit as ourselves, cannot harmonize their movements with ours, and would merely serve to introduce discord and disorder where nature wishes only order and concord.

Accordingly, then, we should all attempt to remain within the specific social circle to which we belong and not seek more contact with others than is required for the proper functioning of the social machine of which each one of us forms a part. Now then, Mr. Editor, I believe that certain persons are remiss in their duty to society in general and to others of their own class and rank in particular. I refer to those gentlemen who, forgetting their obligation to us, their mothers, their sisters, and their relatives, are pleased to attend dances of *grisettes*,[2] where they will certainly not find any understanding of the concerns which correspond to their own station, education, and class. Of course I am far from wishing to deny to any member of my sex, whatever might be her class or station, the physical and moral qualities which characterize these girls. On the contrary, some of the girls whom I observed from the street during such a dance the other evening combined good taste in their dress with ease and gracefulness in their movements, a combination which I could but envy.

It is precisely because of the attractions of these dances that I dare to raise my voice against the young gentlemen of our society who frequent them; apart from the manner in which they affront our honor, in these dances they learn an indescribable way of dancing which certainly is not of the most *comme il faut*, we might say. Among themselves, these dances are called by names so grotesque that I can barely remember them although I have heard them a thousand times from my brother Pepe, who, incidentally, is one of the offenders. So incomprehensible are some of these names—*merengue, cola de pato, de ladrillo, de úcar y bejuco, de pilón, de botella y medio* and others equally incongruous—that I have wearied of seeking them in the Dictionary of the Royal Academy. In addition, the familiarity which these dances encourage and the openness which both sexes observe in dancing them do not satisfy my idea of feminine reserve, for a woman, regardless of her class, should never stray beyond the barrier of prudence which envelops her dignity. Consider, Mr. Editor, the idea of a young woman offering to identify herself (when disguised) to a young man during a masked ball by a pinch. And if this acquaintance begins with a pinch, where will it end? I can testify to this matter of the pinch, for the young man himself dared to relate it to my brother Pepe in my presence. Tell me, Mr. Editor, if I am not correct in condemning the custom, now widespread among young gentlemen, of frequenting those dances. Let the married men go if they wish; that does not interest me as it does not have the same consequence for us. But it is different for the younger men, for all of us young ladies have brothers and relatives among them, and aside from any matter of envy or wounded self-esteem, which in any case we are incapable of feeling, our duty is to watch over that which is ours. I am certain that you will join me in censuring the custom of which I write; as I understand that you are not one of those who enjoy such activities I am sure that these brief notes will serve to enlist your support for our cause and that naturally you will aid us in deterring the young gentlemen from attending dances others than ours. For my part, I promise to do what I can to discourage my friends from dancing with any young man who from now on permits himself to frequent the dance halls of Isabel or Carnicería streets. We

shall see if the threat of such a punishment will not cause them to return
to their duty.

(Signed) *A Ponceña*[3]

□   □   □

(2) Ponce, August 29, 1853
To the Editor, *El Ponceño*[4]

Dear Sir: Also endowed only with my title of "woman," and as a
women wounded by an article printed in no. 61 of the newspaper which
you so sagaciously edit, signed by "A Lady of Ponce," I beg that you
deign to aid me along the difficult journey upon which I am embarked,
both because of my limited abilities and because you have offered to become the protector of *all* of your female readers, most of whom, including this correspondent, are members of the second social class.

I cannot rebut with technical language the comparison of society with
a steam engine which the previous writer made; a poor girl of my class,
who must be occupied with the blessed sewing needle all day and sometimes into the night in order to earn the sustenance of her family, including an aged mother who without her aid might be obliged to beg for
succor elsewhere; what can such a poor girl know, Mr. Editor? Very little. To answer technically one would have to have at least studied me-
chanics, mathematics, physics, and certain other sciences; not having
studied such subjects for lack of the necessary financial resources I can
thus answer only on the basis of common sense, which in any case often
turns out to be correct.

Clearly, society can be compared to a steam engine, but also clearly,
all of an engine's parts and all of its devices function with precision and
accuracy due to the astute combination designed by its manufacturer; if
one part is missing it must be provided, or if one should break or cease
its movement it must be replaced. If society is like a steam engine, then,
people are its parts; as we women are also part of the grand assembly it
follows that the social machine could not function without the part which
we represent. If my father had owned a plantation and a steam engine
with which to elaborate its products, I might have watched its performance and could thus present a more convincing case. But alas; my father never rose above the honorable station of artisan.

In spite of having attended all of the dances at the second-class hall,

Mr. Editor, I have never heard there the expressions *cola de pato, pilón* or the others referred to by the *ponceña* but which I shall not repeat as I find them hardly poetic: inappropriate for utterance by such a lady. In fact I do not believe that a woman composed such peculiar phrases; in addition, the writer failed to take into consideration the harm which he was doing to the very society which he was defending. Our newspaper circulates not only in this town, and readers in the other places where it is received might be expected to form an unflattering judgment of Ponce society. A writer should not only adorn his prose with choice expressions but must also bear in mind the consequences of their use. If he fails to do so he might suffer the same fate as the artist who paints a picture representing all of the vices of society in order to correct them only to find the vices intensified because of the scant garments in which he clothed his figures, despite his heavenly colors and other meritorious touches.

You have attended our dances. What have you seen at them which would cause such ado? People dance there as people usually dance in most island towns; I have always observed a pattern of prudent behavior, and if our dances are frequented by young men moved by jealousy it is because our masked balls are really masked balls, with the liveliness and the antics typical of such diversions. No one who attends our dances would leave disappointed, nor would he feel excluded because of slight attendance, nor because my friends had eight or ten *contradanzas* already promised. This is because my friends, knowing the style and the procedures of masked balls, know that promising eight or ten dances beforehand is not the way a masked ball is conducted.

I do not know the sense in which the writer uses the word *grisettes*, because of the variety of meanings and implications which may be assigned to it. However, no woman (and no man hiding behind a woman's signature) should use language which does not correspond to the writer's station in society, for a person's language is seen as the thermometer of his education. I believe that *grisette* is equivalent to our *manolas* of Madrid: uninhibited working-class girls, just as in Paris the term is applied to the seamstresses who work in such places as dress shops and tailor shops. But as I have observed, the term is also applied with other implications, and I shall explain no further because the concepts of culture which my father instilled in me despite his poverty do not permit me to do so.

The plan outlined by *la ponceña*, of no longer dancing with the young men who have had the pleasure (or who have suffered from the weakness, let us say) of favoring us with their attendance at the Isabel, is of little interest to me—or I should say, of no interest at all. I trust that the ladies have also planned what to do in order to not lose out entirely in the matter. However, I shall simply observe that they will probably dance no more, because all of the young gentlemen, with few exceptions, have enjoyed the order, the enthusiasm, and the taste which have marked these dances, for which all of us offer sincere thanks to the management.

I conclude, Mr. Editor, defender of the weaker sex, by begging you to help me in your accustomed spirit of impartiality to counter the message of the so-called *ponceña*, a message which causes so much damage to all social groups, convinced as I am that you will do this because I have both morality and reason on my side.

Yours most respectfully,
(Signed) *Second Ponceña*

The Dangerous *Danza*

Carlos Peñaranda, "La *danza*," in his *Cartas puerto-riqueñas dirigidas al célebre poeta don Ventura Ruiz Aguilera* (Madrid, 1885). Reprint (San Juan: Editorial El Cemí, 1967), 69-73.[5]

My dear and respected friend: The most noteworthy, the most prevalent, indeed the first element which attracts the attention of the European upon his arrival here is dancing. Dancing attracts our attention both for the great enthusiasm which the sons and daughters of this island feel for it and also for the characteristics which distinguish the native dances from those of other countries.

Leaving aside the dances seen at affairs of certain social rank and official function and also disregarding those seen at public dance halls (which according to a newspaper, nobody of substance would admit to attending), we can without risk of error reduce the general custom of the island to a single kind of dance: the *danza puertorriqueña*.

Soft and tender to the point of being called "merengue"; its pace quick and sensual; its pulse, melodies, and sound sweet and enervating, and with its drum and its *güiro*, both instruments inherited from the Indian race or adopted from the African or perhaps representing a mixture of both. The Puerto Rican *danza*, the most characteristic dance of the Americas, attracts and repels; heats and cools the blood; laughs and cries; enlivens and kills.

Someone has called it a prolonged sigh, a very graphic expression from several points of view, because in the *danza* love moans, the veins ignite, passion becomes aroused and honest virtue trembles, crushed within the arm which encircles the waist. Tremulous is the hand sustained by sensuality; longing is the bosom raised and lowered as by waves incited in a hurricane: the lips enflamed, the eyes moist with emotion, the body moving with the motion of the palm tree rocked by gusts of burning wind howling over the sands.

The *danza* is a chain of soft laments, of lovers' wooings, of voluptuous chords, of soft impressions. The music is seemingly charged with diverse emotions; like a box which is opened it scatters its notes on the wind and spills out its harmonies of tender ambiguities, pain and pleasure, sadness and hope. The soul, suspended between disparate fancies; the heart, irresolute among conflicting sensations: both await a signal which might awaken their fibers, a note which might call out a memory from within. The fretful *güiro* emits its dry and dragging vibrations, giving the orchestra a certain sense of langour, a certain listless desire, a certain indolent eagerness and thirst for soft pleasures. It seems like a murmur of the soul, a cry echoed in the solitude of America's virgin forests: a remote memory which has enlisted music's voice to mock life's agitation; an infinite thirst for pleasures which has not been able to control the rebellious spirit, and cracks that sacred vessel of the soul which protects the perfumes of heavenly loves and celestial desires, now violently scattered by tempestuous winds. Thus that harmonious murmur, if it bears any pure essence at all, bears it in the wings of the tempest's burning winds; thus, that impassioned cry is not the light which illuminates the temple of emotion and the higher life, but a flame which burns and destroys; after consuming everything in its path it adds to the horror of death the even greater horror of darkness.

Much has been written about this dance and long debates have recently taken place in the island press concerning its suitability as a wholesome diversion or its undesirability as leading fatally to misconduct and immorality. I shall not hesitate to express my opinion nor to explain the numberless social and artistic considerations which lead me to see dancing as a very agreeable thing when only the fair sex engages in it but repulsive when the movements produced by the intimate union of a man and a woman seem to call at the very doors of a churlish sensuality.

If to this view are added the details which I enumerated earlier, it will be clear why my opinion must be against this dance. I consider it a corruptor of customs, opposed to all of the great expressions of the soul;

I consider it the spurious daughter of a race which is today strong and virile, called to fulfill great destinies, of a race which needs noble inspirations and continuous inducements to its spirit so that it might project itself fully into the intellectual life of modern times, and not sensual entertainments which parch its forces, constrict its spirit, and detain it on its long road.

It is necessary to elevate the spirit, not debase it. The human spirit must not descend from its high station but acquire the intimate and permanent conscience corresponding to its greatness; intelligence must rise to its throne, not descend to hell hearing like a dirge that music which puts it to sleep and then extinguishes it, which first excites it and then kills it.

And on contemplating those dances in which persons of all social classes become intermixed in their willingness to abandon themselves to the dazzling madness of the licentious *danza*, and upon observing in the streets of San Juan during Carnival those men, those women, those children, sometimes tattered, often ignorant, always unhappy, as with crude contortions they cavort to the measure of a monotonous music; on hearing these strange notes, more likely the product of some inert material than of our century's vivifying and noble spirit, I am sure that all who think, all who love the great and the good will protest in the depths of their conscience, as I do, that sickness of the soul and of the ear, first in the name of art, then in the name of womanhood, and finally in the name of reason and human dignity.

The *Danza*: The Traditional View

Amaury Veray, "La misión social de la danza de Juan Morel Campos," *Revista del Instituto de Cultura Puertorriqueña* 2, no. 5 (October-December 1959): 35-38. Reprinted in *Ensayos sobre la danza puertorriqueña*, Marisa Rosado, comp. (San Juan: Institute of Puerto Rican Culture, 1977), 38-45.

The Puerto Rican *danza* is not as old as some believe it to be. It is not to be found in the opening pages of our nineteenth-century history, and even less should it be sought in earlier times. However, its essential features may have been gestating in our *settecento*, without attaining definite form until it found a favorable environment during the fourth decade of the past century.

Nor is it correct to focus the *danza* exclusively on the figure of Juan

Morel Campos. Besides being historically incorrect, this would be unjust to the other composers who contributed to its development. To arrive at an understanding of the value of the *danza* as it was cultivated by Morel Campos it is also necessary to study the works of the other figures who took part in its evolution.

Juan Morel Campos enters the world of the *danza* around 1875. This period was both critical and fruitful in the process of our historical definition; the *danza* of Morel was born and reached maturity in Ponce, in fact accompanying in parallel fashion the spiritual development of that southern city.

The *danza* reaches maturity in the 1880s, when Ponce was at the vanguard of the political movement in Puerto Rico. The *danza* of the 1880s is as distinctive of Ponce as the architecture of the city's solid houses of sober colors and handsome balconies, surrounded by gardens in their flat, smooth, and otherwise featureless landscapes. The *danza* of Morel Campos is saturated by the atmosphere of Ponce, and displays the defining qualities of that austere, provincial, sober, and defiant Ponce society of the 1880s. Morel's *danza* belongs first to Ponce and only secondly to Puerto Rico, remaining sound and unharmed because it remained untouched by extraneous influences.

The Ponce element in Morel's *danza* was unmistakable, as the type spread out from its birthplace to the rest of the island, always bearing an intrinsic indigenous quality conceived by Morel himself. The attention of the rest of the island's composers was focused on the *danza* of Ponce, although a tradition of *danza* composition had also developed in San Juan, guided by Braulio Dueño Colón, Julián Andino, Casimiro Duchesne, and others. Nevertheless, it was the Ponce *danza* which established the pattern.

It must be recognized, however, that the Ponce *danza* did not begin with Morel but with San Juan-born Manuel Gregorio Tavárez, who years before had become established in Ponce and had given form to the *danza* of that city.

The *danza* was a decisive and extremely important factor in the formation of our psychological profile, and for many years its cultivation was our composers' main concern. Puerto Rican composers wrote music of general character, to be sure, but they sought the seal of Puerto Rican identity in the *danza*. This was the case of Braulio Dueño Colón, Casimiro Duchesne, Heraclio and Federico Ramos, Juan Ríos Ovalle, Angel Mislán, Jaime Pericás, José Quintón, Monsita Ferrer, Jesús Figueroa, Simón Madera, José E. Pedreira, and so many others. Only Arístides

Chavier followed other models, perhaps motivated by a dislike of the *danza*.

The *danza* came to represent the highest goal of Puerto Rican art music. Others of our musical forms have arisen from time to time, but became debilitated or were lost because they were not written down. On the other hand, the *danza* forms part of our literate musical culture and reveals the authentic and characteristic facets of our society throughout its development.

The island's political trajectory serves as a conceptual frame for the *danza*. It would not be difficult to place the *danza* in three basic periods: that of Tavárez, that of Morel Campos, and that of Quintón. Each one of the three composers established a landmark, and we might call the three periods the period of formation, the period of maturity, and the period of consequence or effect. These three periods coincide with three different visions of our political life. First was separatism, a movement which coincided with the period of the *danza's* formation. Second was a period marked by the opposition of two political movements, assimilism and autonomism, a period which coincided with virtually the entire musical production of Juan Morel Campos. Finally, the change of Puerto Rico's political sovereignty in 1898 and the subsequent adjustments coincided with the development of the *danza* at the hands of José Ignacio Quintón. The *danza* of Juan Morel Campos, as we have indicated, corresponds to the period of the assimilist-autonomist controversy in Puerto Rico. For this reason the *danza* left a profound mark on our musical history; indeed, it took possession of our innermost being as it developed and became defined within this framework of contrasting political philosophies.

The *danza* of Morel, itself rooted in the *danzas* of Tavárez, is a worthy heir of the old Spanish *contradanza* and of the Cuban *habanera*, which was brought to Puerto Rico in the retinue of General Aristegui in 1844 and which immediately found a place in our social framework. In this way it came to serve as the most convincing testimony of the flowering of our nineteenth-century colonial society and indeed, of the birth of Puerto Rican society itself. This was a felicitous occurrence: the transformation of of a purely Spanish colonial society into the nucleus of an emergent Puerto Rican society, which was to attain definitive characteristics in the last third of our twentieth century although it had been gestating for some time previously.

The phenomenon which produced the *danza* of Juan Morel Campos is extremely interesting, for it goes beyond the limits of the purely musical to reveal links with general cultural matters: an attractive confluence for Puerto Rican musicians. The *danza* of Juan Morel Campos expresses our feelings and our thoughts; it reveals us as we truly are. Nor is there any point in seeking academic turns of phrase in Morel's *danza,* for it proudly displays the flavor of popular music. To enumerate technical errors which are only of interest from the point of view of musical analysis would be a dry exercise, for Morel's *danza* transcends the field of music. Indeed, Morel's technical inconsistencies provide the undeniable freshness and spontaneity of his *danzas*; they become the expression of a young and impulsive people which is learning to sing without pretension or artifice.

The *danza* of the end of the nineteenth century is the ideal expressive mode for the Puerto Rican society of the period. In it we enveloped ourselves as we discovered the miracle of our own identity; for this reason the *danza* became our most genuine and most authentic form of dance music. Other dance forms brought to Puerto Rico or born in the Antilles always yielded first place to the *danza*, which was the first dance of close contact known to our emergent middle class. Unlike the *contradanza*, the *lancero* and the *rigodón*, dependent on recruiting enough dancers to form the required figures, the *danza* was danced by couples. It was the most intimate dance known at the time.

No less interesting are the factors which contributed to the success of the *danza* in Morel's hands. Tavárez' promising designs went no further than the restricted ambience of the home musicale. However, the development of new patterns of sociability called for the creation of social centers where larger groups might assemble to chat and gossip. The youth of Ponce played a leading role in this development, and dancing became the ideal method for establishing and maintaining informal social relationships between the sexes.

Judging from preserved photographs and orchestra materials, it was at this time that the typically small dance orchestra began to expand, for the type of group which had played *lanceros*, mazurkas, and *rigodóns* now performed *danzas* as well. The *danza* of Morel became solidly established in our public dance halls, while its pleasing and flexible rhythm undoubtedly inspired the creation of new dance steps. The design of the *danza* would reflect the customs of the society which cultivated it, as the introductory section of the old *contradanza* now became the elegant *paseo* during which couples paraded in stately fashion around the floor. The charm and dignity of this promenade imparted grace and elegance to the couples who took part in it, maintained throughout the dance itself and subtly affecting the entire assembly. The inevitable euphonium solo, faithful factor in the *danza* tradition, was to break through the innocent cantilena of simple melody to become the harbinger of instrumental virtuosity in our music. For this reason, orchestras competed in engaging the best available euphonium soloists. Among the most distinguished of these were Angel Mislán Huertas, Domingo Cruz ("Cocolía"), and Juan Morel Campos himself. The *danza* came to be the essential ritual of our social life; the passage through which several generations of Puerto Rican youth would travel: the academy and the judge of our social acumen. It provided the opportunity for discreet flirtation, for the intimate revelation of love's claims, and for the assertion of delicate reproaches. How many tender secrets were revealed while dancing to "De tu lado al paraíso," or "No desconfies," or "Cede a mis ruegos!"

The Puerto Rican *danza* symbolizes the aristocratic bourgeoisie of our society, and the better it is danced the more enjoyable it is. Naturally, some prefer a particular and fondly remembered *danza* above all others, for it may recall love's youthful adventures as well as the ancient links of some sincere friendship of years past. That dream is still alive. The *danza* of Morel Campos preserves the nobility of our Puerto Rican being; it gathers together the most delicate hues of our proprieties, which when united produce a state of enchantment. With it, life gains new value and Puerto Rican womanhood as well, as her femininity becomes ennobled. Some even speak of the beauty of the unattractive, in the context of the ennobling *danza*. The gentleman controls the dance and is responsible for its perfor-mance; he designs the steps, while his attentive partner follows them with scrupulous precision. As the *danza* symbolizes the organization of our society, the gentleman directs the progress of the dance in the same way that he directs the destiny of the home. The woman is the passive element in which are fulfilled the vows of conjugal happiness and where gently rocks the tender consciousness of the future paterfamilias. The *danza* of Morel Campos is the emblem of this society. Its thematic range is vast, extending far beyond romantic fancy. It possesses the felicity of the golden mean, and in it are manifested the values of the Puerto Rican social structure of the period.

The *danzas* of Morel Campos cover the entire range of our insular society, due precisely to the great variety of his works and to the diversity of features which they display. Because of this variety and diversity, we cannot identify Morel as the autobiographical subject of his work; instead, he is perhaps the supreme chronicler of his period. His work is a mural which depicts an entire generation, an entire epoch, and the entire life of a people, and in his music he was able to communicate the broad emotional panorama of that people. Sparse in daily conversation, reserved in his opinions, and disposed toward forming close and firm friendships; we know little of Morel's inner self. This limited knowledge of his personality has given rise to legends, for we freely embellish our cultural dominion and romanticize our existence with grand fantasies. In addition, the thematic range of Morel's work invites the weaving of romantic visions of the composer's own life and personality.

Morel's works, strung together, form a rosary of loving phrases upon which clever people have created poetic fantasies. Nevertheless, these titles do not always suit the spirit of the texts, nor much less the rhythmic base of the music. To illustrate this statement, we might cite the case of "Maldito amor,"or "El asalto," or "De tu lado al paraíso." In all of these a sentimental lyricism is definitely noted, in which the musical phrase consistently rules the *danza*. Morel's *danzas* have a unique foundation and an equally unique design aside from his magnificent rhythmical combinations, his admirable management of dynamics, and above all, his mastery of harmonic diversity. At random one might choose "Sueño de amor," composed in the *año terrible* of 1887;[6] "Felices días;" "Tormento;" "Ausencia;" "Tuya es mi vida," "Todo corazón;" "Bendita seas;" or" Tu imagen," among so many others. All are conceived within different rhythmic schemes. In addition, the melodic contour of each one is unique although the design always calls for an ascending melodic line. Among all of our *danza* composers Morel Campos had the most genuine and most extraordinary grasp of musical architecture. This was possible because of his mastery of the dramatic element and of his predilection for the unexpected. It is enough to remember "Di que me amas," a magnificent example of this technique. On the other hand we find a curious resemblance among some of his *danzas*. "Tormento" and "Candorosa" are twin sisters, and we cannot determine which work was derived from the other. It is possible to conceive of both works as resulting from the same flash of artistic euphoria. In addition, Morel clearly enjoyed using identical rhythmic schemes in different *danzas*, as is the case of "Candorosa" and the eloquent "No desconfíes."

For Morel Campos the *danza* did not necessarily follow any particular pattern. Indeed it could not, for his type of *danza* stands above any abstract constraint. At times a rhythmic profile provides the basis for melodic development. The same might occur with the delineation of the central sections of a work, for Morel was interested in the absolute unity of the *danza*. His works transcended the severe restrictions of the older design, and we have found no examples of it among his compositions: not even in such early works as "Maldito amor," dating from 1884, the year of Tavárez' death.[7] "Maldito amor" thus provides early evidence of Morel's originality.

We know of no work earlier than "El sopapo" (1870), of which we have only the title. In "Maldito amor" we already see the force of the composer's artistic personality: spontaneous, dramatic, and expressive. "Maldito amor" represents a rhythmic revolution, for here we find rhythm based on patterns of accentuation. In this period begins the conceptual spiral of Morel's music, which has so enriched our musical history.

It is important to realize that although Morel Campos borrowed the Tavárez model of the *danza* he assumed no responsibility for perpetuating it. In fact, Morel's *danzas* represent a reaction to it. The Morel Campos *danza* is a romantic display very different from Tavárez' works: a display which emulates the boisterous turn which our world of ideas was about to take. The dramatic impact produced by Morel's *danzas* was so powerful that his works absolutely dominated the field. Furthermore, the *danza* of Morel Campos became the seal and symbol of Puerto Rican society, and to invoke it is to perceive the values of this society.

As is to be expected, musical developments accompanied the unfolding of social transformations in nineteenth-century Puerto Rico, but then music would not be music if it were not part of this union.

With the *danzas* of Morel Campos was born the familiar expression *aire de danza*, or "in the style of the *danza*." But why *aire de danza*? Did the *danza* not already possess a satisfactory musical notation? Perhaps what was wanted was a kind of indication that might preserve a living musical tradition for which standard musical notation was not appropriate. What then is meant by the expression *aire de danza*? I believe that it simply indicates a way of transmitting a message, drawing upon the stylistic resources of the folk, which may make possible the communion of a people despite the fact of their physical separation.

The *danza* of Morel Campos was the product of many other factors as well, and the most important of these was undoubtedly the political condition which is reflected there. What insistently emerges is the music's Puerto Rican quality; perhaps what is expressed rather intensely in Tavárez becomes calm resolution in Morel. In these works the melodic contour, in spite of its great stylistic variety, flows spontaneously and free of tension. Morel's melodic flow is polished and serene, devoid of worry or concern.

The dramatic touches which unexpectedly occur in many of Morel's *danzas* are relevant to the real life drama which began in our lives just at the culmination of his career. The instability of our political and social world is perfectly portrayed in the *danzas* of Morel. For this reason his melodies are flighty and mercurial; when we try to capture their essence they have already escaped. This eloquent nervousness characterizes the greatest moments in all of his danzas. Then, after carrying a musical phrase to the highest and purest levels he abandons it because it no longer interests him or because in the distance he hears another phrase which pleases him more. His music is an unrelenting desire to capture beauty; an unending frenzy of endeavor. Morel Campos ceases to be a musician to become the poet of the musical ideal; from this spark emerges Morel's unique sense of musical form.

Morel's sense of form is imperishable, for it illuminates a moment of our history. We are still plagued by the same doubts, the same problems, the same insecurities and even the same resigned acquiescence which are sensed in the *danzas* of Morel Campos. Although we are pained by it, we still bear part of that epoch today. However, it seems to me improper to adulterate and falsify the *danza* of Morel in isolated performances; this music is still the highest exemplar of our present spiritual condition.

The *danza* has left the realm of dance music to become an art form: a purely Puerto Rican art. Who knows; perhaps having passed through these categories it might become a form of art song. Why should it not be said? It is a message which arrives made song, and which nests in its essence the spirit of that same inconstant, flighty, submissive, and humble cadence which delineates the profile of our personality. Morel's *danza* constituted the baptism of our organized society. If we consider these details, it is not improper to speak of its social mission. It has been at our side constantly. This leads us to believe that we are all children of the Puerto Rican *danza* and especially of the *danza* of Morel Campos because of our felicitous blood relation and because we have all grown up, consciously or unconsciously, in the warmth of its maternal serenity.

The *Danza:*
A Sociopolitical View

Angel G. Quintero Rivera, "Ponce, la danza y lo nacional: apuntes para una sociología de la música puertorriqueña," *Música* (Havana), no. 107 (January-June 1986): 5-21.[8]

Many foreigners are surprised and some Puerto Ricans are irritated by the fact that a *danza*, "La borinqueña," is our national anthem. The national anthems of most countries are marches, representing the most stirring form of military music. But military force has always been a foreign element in Puerto Rico and sometimes has even been directly opposed to what Puerto Rico wished to be. It is also significant that in spite of the fact that *danzas* comprise a small proportion of today's vast and rich production of music, "Verde luz," a *danza* by Antonio Cabán Vale ("El topo"), has for many become the anthem of contemporary Puerto Rico. How and why has the *danza* acquired such significance within our cultural panorama?

Some writers on musical subjects, pursuing the type of cultural analysis which bears the official stamp of the Institute of Puerto Rican Culture, conceive the *danza* as our principal national music because it incorporates elements of the three ethnic strands which formed our population. The texts and melodies come mainly from the Spanish tradition; the rhythm displays marked African influences, and the use of the *güiro* is offered as proof of native Taíno Indian influence. However, this same combination of influences might be claimed for the *seis*, the *plena*, the *merengue* or, indeed, for most of the music of the Hispanic Caribbean. Then why is our anthem a *danza* and not a *seis*? Could it be a matter of proportion among these different elements, with the *danza* providing the most representative or most perfect formula?[9] Or should we not seek other lines of analysis?

To begin to address these questions I believe it important to approach the social world in which the *danza* took form and flourished: the world of Ponce, the island's second largest city, in the second half of the nineteenth century. It is important to first point out that during the first centuries of Spanish colonization a rigid division had developed between San Juan and "the island." San Juan represented the presence of officialdom and colonialism while the rest of Puerto Rico represented something of a refuge from them. Until the eighteenth century the economy of "the island" remained essentially one of subsistence, in a world and a region of growing international trade. Free of the official scrutiny of San Juan officialdom, this trade became channeled through extraofficial means: through contraband, whose importance is frequently noted in documents of the period.

At the end of the eighteenth century and particularly at the beginning of the nineteenth, Spain encouraged the development of commercial agriculture in Puerto Rico: the cultivation of products which might be sold abroad, mainly coffee and sugarcane products. With the export duties received from such trade, Spain hoped to realize financial benefit from Puerto Rico and thus support its military garrison in San Juan.

The colonial power thus encouraged the transformation of a peasant subsistence economy to an economy based on haciendas, plantations producing commodities for export. In addition, Spain declared intense war on contraband trade in order to collect the export duties. Commerce became centralized in several coastal towns where official customs offices were established; contraband trade, spread out along the coasts, was replaced by officially recognized commerce channeled mainly through San Juan, Ponce, and Mayagüez.

San Juan was the main importing city, while Ponce and Mayagüez became the principal export centers.[10] San Juan represented Spanish officialdom both civil and military; the city increasingly controlled an import trade which was in fact tied to this officialdom itself.[11] Meanwhile, Ponce and Mayagüez became business centers for the agricultural exporting class of plantation owners, *hacendados*. As Ponce and Mayagüez were agricultural business centers, urban-rural distinctions were much less marked here than in San Juan. Indeed, these centers were the partners of agriculture, not its adversary as the fortress city of San Juan came to be.[12]

Hacendados were a highly contradictory class, as contradictory as the hacienda economy itself. On one hand this economy existed for the production of commodities: of products for sale. The highest development of the mercantile economy is capitalism, and the developing hacienda economy leaned toward this model. But on the other hand the hacienda economy was based on pre-capitalistic forms of exploitation of labor,[13] including slavery and above all, servile or semi-feudal types of relationship. That is, hours of work were not exchanged for a salary as in a capitalist system; instead, the peasant's labor was secured by other means. Such means included permitting him access to the land through share-cropping arrangements, or by securing his labor by such coercive laws as the *libreta* (work-record book), or through such intermediate forms as payment in kind, or through perpetual indebtedness to the plantation store, or by payment in chits instead of money.[14] These relationships made this economy an essentially feudal one although its development always tended toward the capitalist model, the project of its dominant class. In this sense the *hacendados* formed a manorial class aspiring to attain a capitalist role.

This class was contradictory in another way as well. The hacienda economy was originally encouraged by Spain, but at the same time the colonial control of commerce set limits to its development. Because of these limits, a class originally allied with Spanish colonialism as its defender came to oppose that same colonialism. This ambivalent opposition manifested itself in autonomism, the principal political position of the *hacendado* class at the end of the nineteenth century.

As their domination of the life of production progressed, *hacendados* attempted to gain control of the rest of the economy, which was governed by merchants, and of the island's general social and public life, ruled by colonial officialdom. But in order to do this, they needed the acquiescent support of a majority of the island population. In an effort to present their own interests as the interests of the broader society, *hacendados* developed a policy of Puerto Rican affirmation through their Autonomist Party. In fashioning this view, existing social conflicts became defined as opposition between native Puerto Ricans and peninsular Spaniards.[15] The bourgeois-manorial tension inherent in this ideology generated a contradictory national vision: a paternalistic concept of the island population as a great all-encompassing family: a stratified family to be sure, ruled by "the father of us all"—the planter class—but a family after all, and one which included the "honorable sons of toil."

It was no coincidence that the stronghold of the Autonomist Party was Ponce, the island's main exporting center, which had one foot in the country (the hacienda) and which aspired toward national importance. The party's most important general assemblies were held in Ponce and it was in Ponce that the party's newspaper was published: *La Democracia*, which became Puerto Rico's leading periodical.

Nor was it by coincidence that it was in Ponce, stronghold of the social class which had national aspirations, that the musical form was born which most of our writers on musical subjects consider to be our first national music.[16] Lamps were installed in Ponce's main plaza, the Plaza de las Delicias, in 1864, allowing the inauguration there of public concerts. Beginning with Tavárez the island's most innovative composers began to move to Ponce, weary of composing military and ecclesiastical music for San Juan.[17] And in the 1880s, the decade of the consolidation of the political party through which native planters would pursue their struggle for power, the *danzas* of Juan Morel Campos flowered: the product of Ponce's greatest composer.[18] The "Very Seignorial City of Ponce" was the stronghold of a socioeconomic class increasing in importance, and to all real effects—cultural, political, economic, and social—Ponce was also the alternative capital of Puerto Rico.

But the *hacendados* didn't compose *danzas*, and their nationalistic struggle only partly explains the *danza's* rise. Like other towns and cities, Ponce was populated not only by planters, merchants, functionaries, and officials but also by skilled workers: carpenters, masons, dressmakers, tailors, barbers, cigarmakers, printers, . . . in short, by craftsmen, by artisans. It was from the world of the Ponce artisans, and naturally through their relation with other social classes, that the *danza* arose.[19]

Most artisans were blacks or mulattos. Some had been skilled plantation slaves and had moved to the city following their emancipation, while others had lived as free blacks. In a society which slavery had left deeply marked by racism, one of the most important of the island artisans' early battles was the struggle for dignity; for the recognition of their civil existence; for their acceptance as persons and as citizens. The artisans' struggle was later to become radicalized, acquiring an independent and defiant character at the end of the nineteenth century and especially at the beginning of the twentieth.[20] But at the time of the rise of the *danza* the battle for their dignity was still being waged within the frame established by the planters. The *hacendados'* concept of the "great all-encompassing Puerto Rican family," very different from the position of the island's Spanish conservatives, indicated the acceptance of the "honorable sons of toil" as members—although lesser members —of the community. The Autonomist Party defended public education and the extension of suffrage. And clear evidence exists of the participation of artisans—subordinate participation, to be sure—in reform movements launched by the planters.[21]

It is also significant that it was in Ponce, bastion of reform movements, that the first artisans' newspaper of which we have notice was published: *El Artesano* (1874). The paper's masthead bore the identification "Periódico Republicano Federal" when federated republicanism was precisely the rallying cry of the *hacendados* in their struggle for an autonomous government. It is also highly significant that before the advent in 1897 of the *Ensayo Obrero,* marking the radical transformation to an independent labor movement, four of the island's six preserved craft and labor newspapers were published in Ponce. All sought the recognition of labor as worthy of respect, but within the frame of the liberal movement fostered by the *hacendados*.

The musical analysis of the *danza* is highly revealing, for it was a form of music produced by artisans just at the time of their fight for recognition. In great measure the *danza* is a music *of* artisans, but produced *for hacendados*; the music thus forms part of the relation between the two classes. It is an authentically popular expression which nonetheless bears the stamp of the *hacendado* hegemony. In the *danza*, several folk elements drawn from the *seis* of the countryside and the *bomba* of the plantation, while also receiving obvious Cuban and Spanish influences,[22] become transformed into a sophisticated kind of salon music which the *hacendados* might smugly dance in their exclusive casinos.[23] The institution of the *bastonero* disappeared during the early development of the *danza*: the cane-wielding dancing-master who dictated the steps and figures of the old *contradanza*.[24] In this way each dancing couple enjoyed a great degree of freedom. However, the *danza* also retained something of the formality of the older figured dances, thus manifesting the bourgeoisie-aristocracy tension which marked the hacendados' contradictory campaign.

The friction between San Juan and the countryside and the foreign character of the capital's dominant class, identified as it was with the Spanish government, were of no help in the formation of an integrating hegemony with San Juan at the head. Such official celebrations as *fiestas patronales* were enlivened by the alternation of military bands with musical groups formed by artisans and by rural peasants: the urban populace, dancing until dawn, amused itself by "obstructing the work of the poor *jíbaros* as they arrived at the market with their loads of produce."[25]

The character of Ponce, on the other hand, favored a kind of stratified cultural integration. Ponce was the urban capital of a rural world which embraced Puerto Rico's three main agricultural elements: the slave-holding plantation, the manorial hacienda and the independent peasantry. As we have seen, Ponce was the center of a class which aspired to dominance, a class which through the services and the commerce of the port tied these different forms of rural life to the city. Ponce's sociological characteristics, then, made possible the development of an integrating hegemony: an integration earned for the planters by the artisan class in its effort to gain recognition.

The *danza's* characteristic rhythmic figure of quarter-note triplets within the traditional mold of binary meter (the much debated "elastic triplet"), relieved the rhythmic monotony of the European dance music of the period by introducing the flavor of an African rhythmic heritage.[26] In the *bomba* dance, our most important musical reminiscence of the slaveholding plantation, for example, the rhythmic element is so important that the melody accompanies the percussion instead of the reverse.[27] The *danza* assimilated this fundamental role of rhythm, not on the principal level as in the *bomba* but discreetly, without ever competing with or dominating the melody. This fundamental rhythmic function is subtly attained harmonically in the *danza*: through a second melodic voice which outlines harmonic progressions through rhythmic figures. Because of this adaptation the basic rhythmic pulse is no longer percussive: it is sustained not by the drum but by the euphonium or baritone horn, a band instrument of the brass family whose timbre (by no coincidence) most closely resembles that of the drum itself. Describing the euphonium, the instrument played by Juan Morel Campos himself, a writer has pointed out, "We must take this humble instrument into serious consideration, for it is the point of departure for any serious study which intends to examine the harmony of the *danza*."[28]

To assign an important rhythmic role to the drum, an instrument identified with the singing of slaves, in music to be played in ballrooms "of the highest category" was of course unimaginable. The artisans camouflaged the rhythm harmonically, by assigning it to the "humble" euphonium.[29]

This camouflage was so subtle and so successful that even one of the foremost Puerto Rican musicians of the end of the century, Braulio Dueño Colón (the classist perspective of whose *Canciones escolares* awaits examination) was moved to point out, in an essay which was awarded a prize by the Ateneo Puertorriqueño in 1914:

> We cannot deny that for a time our *danza* deteriorated sadly due to the faulty artistic taste of certain composers and orchestra conductors who incorporated elements of the African *bomba* dance, forcing upon the *danza* a grotesque and therefore ugly rhythm.
>
> Fortunately, the exquisite taste of artists like Tavárez, [Heraclio] Ramos and [Morel] Campos prevailed and the native *danza* recovered the gracious and subtle rhythm which had previously characterized it.[30]

Even so, as Dueño could not completely hide his "musical whiteness," he later refers to the triplet as "the faulty rhythmic relation between the melody and the accompaniment," advocating that this "structural defect" be corrected.[31]

It was by way of this "structural defect" that the euphonium introduced into the grand salon, as accompaniment in the *danza*, basic forms of several of our folk music traditions. The euphonium's countermelody became a necessary part of what was then called the *merengue*, the section of the *danza* which followed the introductory *paseo*, for it established a rhythm which itself sustained a harmony part, as a second and complementary voice in the musical texture.[32] Through the euphonium part's extraordinary integration of musical elements the *danza* became a polyphonic form, displaying a texture of several simultaneous melodic lines—a highly sophisticated type of music—at a time when European salon music was almost completely dominated by the homophonic texture generated by a single melodic voice accompanied by chordal or arpeggiated harmonic figurations.[33] It is significant that the Puerto Rican *danza* borrows this polyphonic texture from the music of the countryside: the *seis*, in which the *cuatro*, accompanying the voice with a highly varied countermelody, accomplishes startling polyphonic feats. What was new in the *danza* was that the polyphonic activity also generated the rhythm.

The euphonium, nevertheless, is a subtle instrument. Despite its fundamental importance in the *danza* as the instrument which bestows upon it its very character, it always remains subordinate to the violins and the clarinet. These carry the principal melody while the euphonium discreetly supports them. Thus the euphonium in the *danza* symbolizes and manifests the worker-artisan ideology of the time. This ideology sees work as the center of life in society, but subordinate to the authority of the planter and professional classes. The most which the euphonium can attain in the *danza* is to carry the melody in only one of the four sections of the *merengue*, the part of the work which is danced by couples, and in the third section at that. This is the case, for example, in such *danzas* as "Sara," by Angel Mislán and "Impromptu," by Luis R. Miranda. It is important to not overlook the melodic design of the euphonium solo in the third danced section of the piece, whose similarities with the melodic function of the *cuatro* in the *seis* are again evident although still disguised by the radical change in instrumental timbre. As in the case of the drum, it was impossible at the time to introduce the unsophisticated *cuatro* into the music regularly performed at a genteel casino; musical artisans therefore slipped its tradition into the casino by way of the euphonium.

The introduction of the humble *güiro* at the middle of the nineteenth century, while "rather blasphemous,"[34] was gradually accepted, probably because of its discreet function of simply reinforcing, not establishing, the rhythmic pattern of the music. The *danza*, then, is a sophisticated tribute paid by subordinate classes to the dominant group. For this reason, the dominant class could reasonably identify it with its own culture as "national music." Our analysis of the *danza* thus illustrates the artisans' great potential for national integration. However, this potential was curtailed, as the music itself illustrates, by its being absorbed within the artisans' struggle for the dignity of its recognition as a civil force, and by the *hacendado* class having itself paternalistically absorbed this recognition.

For this reason many Puerto Ricans harbor contradictory sentiments regarding the *danza* today. We definitely enjoy the elegant musical beauty of this tribute by the people, although its servile character might occasionally and quite correctly annoy us.

As the artisans' political movements freed themselves of the *hacendados'* domination, developing their own ideologies and their own independent organizations, the *danza* fell into neglect. At the beginning of the present century the cultural presence of this class became channeled within the broader Puerto Rican labor movement and its struggles, overcoming the servile character of its previous aspiration to recognition and respectability. The *danza* then took refuge in rural folklore. In this way an originally urban form of music gradually changed its character, being kept alive by the traditional rural ensembles of *trovador, cuatro* and guitar. The disappearance of the *hacendado* class in the 1930s also had an effect on the *danza*. As the classes whose relation had established the social framework for the *danza* disappeared or became transformed, then, the genre itself acquired new meanings. In its decline the *danza* became rural music, but in the context of a rural population becoming steadily more urbanized in slums and workers' districts in Puerto Rico and in New York City as well. It is in the tradition of this second emergence of the *danza* that "Verde Luz" must be considered. Here, the servile character of the nineteenth century form becomes transformed into political defiance within a bucolic—though rebellious—idealization of our national society.

Puerto Rican popular music has taken a different course. Tremendously creative, it is still developing new meanings and new forms of expression. In the eighth decade of the twentieth century we can still enjoy the extraordinary music of the *danza*, while recognizing that our national music now flows in other channels. And it is mainly in the dancing and the music of *salsa*, extraordinarily developed musically, that we find our future national anthems.

Methodological Epilogue

During recent decades the Puerto Rican national struggle has reincorporated the idea of popular social conflict which certain important fighters of the early labor movement admirably attempted to impart. Among these were typographer Ramón Rivera Rosa; tailor and tobacco worker Manuel Francisco Rojas; Bernardo Vega, tobacco worker who migrated to New York City; and later the Socialist social worker Carmen Rivera de Alvarado; drivers' leader Francisco Colón Gordiany; barber Isabelino "Pucho" Marzán and many others including the Communist cane cutter and maximum leader of the Puerto Rican workers' movement of the 1940s, Juan Sáez Corales.

In parallel fashion, recognizing and supposedly supporting this view, there has been a recent attempt to distinguish the national phenomenon and class conflict as separable quantities, both strategically and conceptually. In the present essay I have attempted to illustrate, through the analysis of one of our symbols (the anthem, and in its musical form the *danza*), that culture is an all-encompassing phenomenon and that the Puerto Rican national question is inseparable from the dynamic of social classes.[35]

The traditional classist analysis of cultural phenomena frequently falls into an unproductive kind of economic inquiry, which the present essay's examination of the *danza* calls into question. Through the study of a concrete example I have challenged the type of analysis which examines social classes as if they possessed specific characteristics susceptible to *definition* and numeration and in which social phenomena are seen as *reflections* of these characteristics. I have intended to show that social classes are not really *things* but *relations*. These are the relationships which arise among persons because of shared, differing, or antagonistic positions in the structure or the patterns of organization which have formed individuals in their struggle to humanize nature, i.e., to produce an economic product, in order to survive and reproduce. The focus of such analysis, then, is on those relationships which constitute the daily life of work and living together and on the human struggles which are undertaken for the purpose of changing these relationships.

In this context, I consider it an error to postulate cultural phenomena as "representing" specific social classes; such phenomena are rather part of a broad and complex conglomerate of relationships *of* classes or *between* classes. And for the analysis of a particular cultural product, the *danza*, for example, I consider it essential to place it within that *dynamic* of relationships.

For this reason I have argued that the *danza* cannot be considered simply a music of the planter class, nor simply a music of the artisans who created and performed it. Instead, it was a music produced within the complex relation between these classes, or rather, within the complex historical *dynamic* which the complex relationship between these classes experienced as well as the entire complex of social relations existing in nineteenth century Puerto Rico.

Some *danzas* might (or might not) "reflect" the world of the *hacendados*, or might (or might not) "reflect" the aspirations of the artisans. But as a cultural phenomenon, as a musical genre elevated to the stature of a national symbol, the *danza* is much more than any possible "reflection." It is an artistic product framed within the dynamic of class relations. These relations imply subordinate and dominant positions, complex mutual concessions and contradictory attempts to subvert the very meaning of the relationships.

Cultural analysis in terms of class is complex but revealing, and the present attempt, clearly preliminary, is guided by the hope of interesting other Puerto Ricans in this type of task. This type of analysis requires the meticulous search for new sources. It also requires constant discourse among sources, cultivated and disciplined human imagination, and our own theoretical reflections.[36]

Notes

1. *El Ponceño* (Ponce) 2, no. 61 (27 August 1853): 2-3.

2. Light-hearted working girls, although other connotations have been known. See the following letter.

3. "A Lady of Ponce." It is quite possible that this letter, as well as the following one and others regarding the same subject, was written as part of an elaborate joke by Felipe Conde, the newspaper's editor.

4. *El Ponceño* (Ponce) 2, no. 62 (3 September 1853): 5-6. This letter, as well as the previous one and many others regarding the same subject, may also be seen in Socorro Girón, *Ramón C.F. Caballero, "Recuerdos de Puerto Rico" y la polémica del merengue* (Ponce, P.R.: the author, 1984), 196-220.

5. Carlos Peñaranda (1848-1908) was a poet, playwright, essayist, colonial administrator, and a keen and outspoken observer, as well as an avid exponent of the abolition of slavery. He was in Puerto Rico from 1878 to 1888 as a fiscal officer of the colonial government, later serving in important posts in the Philippine Islands. Peñaranda's essays in the form of letters dealing with life and the arts in Puerto Rico were first published in *El Agente* (San Juan) between

1878 and 1880. The present essay was untitled in the 1885 Madrid edition, with the title given here as in the 1967 edition.

6. The reference is to "El año terrible del 87: sus antecedentes y sus consecuencias," a celebrated essay by Antonio S. Pedreira (San Juan, 1937) which described the *componte*, a period of extreme governmental suppression of the autonomist movement in Puerto Rican politics, occurring in 1887.

7. A typographical error. Tavárez died in 1883.

8. (Ed.) This material can also be seen, considerably expanded, as Chapter 6 in the author's *¡Salsa, sabor y control! Sociología de la música "tropical"* (Mexico City and Madrid: Siglo Veintiuno Editores, 1998), 252-99. Unless otherwise indicated, notes are by the author of this essay.

9. Applying this type of analysis, Tomás Blanco argued that the *plena*, not the *danza*, should be deemed our national music, for he considered the *danza* too European, a hothouse plant. See his "Elogio de la plena," *Revista del Ateneo Puertorriqueño* 1, no. 1 (January-March 1935): 97-106.

10. See, for example, J.L. de Vizcarrondo's notes to his edition of André Pierre Ledru, *Viaje a la isla de Puerto-Rico en el año 1797* (San Juan: Imp. Militar de J. González, 1863), 69.

11. On the pro-Spanish alliance of bureaucrats and merchants, see the writings of a leading *hacendado* opposed to this alliance: Francisco Mariano Quiñones, *Conflictos económicos* (Mayagüez: Tip. Comercial, 1888) and *Historia de los Partidos Reformista y Conservador en Puerto Rico* (Mayagüez: Tip. Comercial, 1889).

12. See Albert E. Lee, *An Island Grows: Puerto Rico, 1873-1942* (San Juan: A. E. Lee and Sons, 1963), 11, 67, 68. Lee was born in Ponce as the descendant of English persons who had arrived from the Lesser Antilles. His book offers vivid descriptions of the differences between Ponce and San Juan. Ponce was cosmopolitan, liberal, free thinking, modern; San Juan Catholic, Spanish, conservative.

13. To explain the reasons for this would unduly extend the present essay. However, I have attempted this in previous publications, for example in the first of a series of articles published under the general title "La clase obrera y el proceso político en Puerto Rico," *Revista de Ciencias Sociales* (Río Piedras) 18, no. 1-2 (June 1974): 145-200.

14. A description of the period's economic mechanisms by the present author can be seen in Angel G. Quintero Rivera and Lydia Milagros González, *La otra cara de la historia*, Vol. 1 (San Juan: Centro para el Estudio de la Realidad Puertorriqueña, 1984), Section 2.

15. For greater detail and reference to primary sources, see my *Conflictos de clase y política en Puerto Rico* (San Juan: Huracán-CEREP, 1976).

16. See Amaury Veray, "Vida y desarrollo de la danza puertorriqueña" (1956) and essays by other authors in *Ensayos sobre la danza puertorriqueña*, Marisa Rosado, ed. (San Juan: Instituto de Cultura Puertorriqueña, 1977).

17. It is significant that a foreign musician of the stature of Louis Moreau Gottschalk would also choose to live in Ponce. (Ed.: Gottschalk and the adolescent soprano Adelina Patti spent several weeks concertizing in Ponce between November 1857 and January 1858. See "Baile" in the present anthology.)

18. Amaury Veray, "La misión social de la danza de Juan Morel Campos" (1959) in Rosado, *Ensayos*, explicitly ties the political rise of Ponce to the *danza*, and the latter to Puerto Rican national identity.

19. Some writers have attempted to identify the first *danza*, for example Cecilio R. Font, *Cosas de la danza de Puerto Rico* (Madrid: Artes Gráficas Ibarra, 1970), which explores the formation of the genre as a process that continued from the 1840s until the 1870s. If they were not part of the history of a genre which itself was taking form as a national symbol, the first *danzas* would remain as individual artistic innovations. However, the formation of the *danza* as a genre was a broader musical process in which innumerable musicians participated: composers and performers in constant interaction, particularly in the popular genres. Carpentier, in *La música en Cuba* (México: FCE, 1946), 105, correctly describes the basic forms of Cuban music as "patterns of execution which are later transferred to paper."

20. See Gervasio García, "El casino de artesanos: del rigodón a la huelga," in García and Quintero, *Desafío y solidaridad: breve historia del movimiento obrero puertorriqueño* (San Juan: Huracán-CEREP, 1982), 19-21 and Rubén Dávila Santiago, "El derribo de las murallas y 'El porvenir de Borinquen,'" *CEREP-Cuadernos, Investigación y Análisis* 8 (February 1983).

21. For more details and sources see Angel Quintero Rivera, "Socialista y tabaquero," *Revista Sin Nombre* 7, no. 4 (March 1978).

22. It is not appropriate to the present study to discuss the complicated international tangle of influences which converge in the type of Caribbean music of which the Puerto Rican *danza* forms part. The Cuban author Natalio Galán has written on this subject: *Cuba y sus sones* (Valencia: Pre-Textos, 1983). Especially see Chap. VI, "La contradanza sin contra," which, however, concerns Cuban music only. Here, Galán examines the formation of the genre as a process, and forcefully proves the importance of mulattos and free blacks in the development of this musical tradition. Alejo Carpentier had previously argued the same point, in his *La música en Cuba* (1946). Cristóbal Díaz Ayala, *Música cubana del areyto a la nueva trova* (San Juan: Edit. Cubanacán, 1981), 38, refers specifically to the customary association of musicians with artisans' skills.

23. Veray, "La misión social, " 41, explores this dual character of the *danza*. He points out that it was "the first dance of intimate character known to our nascent bourgeoisie" (referring to the class which I refer to as *hacendados*), having mentioned the *danza's* "popular flavor" only a few lines before. (Ed.: casinos were not gambling establishments but social clubs, with a certain level of social, economic and racial exclusiveness implied.)

24. Specifically, in 1839. See Ernesto Juan Fonfrías, *Apuntes sobre la danza puertorriqueña* (San Juan: Instituto de Cultura Puertorriqueña, 1967), 3. Galán, *Cuba*, 137, also points out the importance of the couple in the development of the Cuban *danza* as part of the period's "modernizing individualism."

25. *Crónica de San Juan o sea descripción de las fiestas con que la ciudad de Puerto Rico ha celebrado a su Santo Patrón en el año de 1864* (San Juan: Imp. del Comercio, 1864), 43.

26. Galán, *Cuba*, 283, identifies for the bolero, in relation to the *contradanza*, a change from triple meter to duple, taking place around 1840. This is seen as a phenomenon of Caribbean "mulattoization," for it allows greater flexibility of accentuation and therefore syncopated cadences, relieving rhythmic monotony.

27. John Storm Roberts, *Black Music of Two Worlds* (New York: Morrow, 1974), along with many other writers, emphasizes the primary role of rhythm in African and Afro-American traditions.

28. Antonio Mirabal, *Próceres del arte: Juan Morel Campos* (Ponce: Oficina Municipal de Historia, 1956), 28.

29. This kind of camouflage was also practiced in the Cuban *danza*, but with other instruments and in other ways. See Galán, *Cuba*, 135, and Carpentier, *La música*, 112.

30. "Estudio de la danza puertorriqueña," reprinted in Rosado, *Ensayos*, 17.

31. Dueño, "Estudio" in Rosado, *Ensayos*, 22. In my opinion the cited writings of Font and Veray correctly defend the triplet figuration.

32. Francis Bebey, *Musique de L'Afrique* (Paris: Horizons de France, 1969) describes as an African tradition the search for and creation of instruments capable of performing melody and percussion simultaneously.

33. Citing an 1865 description, Galán, *Cuba*, 166, notes the European disagreement with the idea of polyphony in the Cuban *danza*.

34. Fonfrías, *Apuntes*, 4.

35. I have explored this relation in a previous study devoted to a very different subject: "Notes on Puerto Rican National Development: Class and Nation in a Colonial Context," *Marxist Perspectives* 9 (Spring 1980): 10-30.

36. Among a wide range of writings whose consideration may help us to function more productively in the relation between research and analysis in dealing with cultural processes, I may recommend two that have been particularly stimulating to me: *The Poverty of Theory and Other Essays* (New York: Monthly Review Press, 1978) by the historian E.P. Thompson and *Problems in Materialism and Culture* (London: Verso, 1980) by the novelist and cultural analyst Raymond Williams.

5

THE TWENTIETH CENTURY

The twentieth century coincided roughly with the present period of United States sovereignty over Puerto Rico, which began with military occupation during the Spanish American War (July 1898). Civil government soon succeeded the military, and later political innovations provided Puerto Rico with steadily greater degrees of internal self government and civil power. But the die was cast; Puerto Rico has now been part of the United States for more than a century, and its musical and artistic fortunes (along with those of educational, economic, political, legal, and military realms) have been increasingly tied to those of the U.S. mainland.

The adjustments have not always been easy. Early disappointments were described by Fernando Callejo in 1915, as island musicians discovered that the new government was not interested in preserving traditional European patterns of state subvention of the arts. Other writers, such as Arístides Chavier and Trinidad Padilla de Sanz, were perhaps more conscious of broader currents in musical culture, pleading for musical training in the schools and for a wider view of the musical art than was current in Puerto Rico in the early part of the century. Echoing U.S. New Deal practices of a decade before, the insular government became involved in the arts during the 1940s with the creation of a short-lived symphony orchestra and a "symphonette," while since the 1950s few island artistic initiatives have not drawn upon government aid, both insular and federal, in one way or another.

An important musical initiative of the 1950s was the creation by the insular government of the annual Puerto Rico Casals Festival, honoring the great Catalan cellist Pablo Casals and motivated by concepts of industrial development and international tourism. However, just as had occurred in 1898 with the transfer of the island's political sovereignty to the United States, the procedures and policies of the extremely powerful Casals Festival management were not universally perceived as a great blessing. Some views on that subject, reflecting debates taking place at the time of their circulation, may be seen in this section.

Meanwhile, and beginning in the 1920s, Puerto Rican popular music and musicians had begun to make a mark in the wider world of international commercial music.[1] The songs of Rafael Hernández became known and admired worldwide, while Puerto Rican musicians became completely and creatively integrated into the vigorous musical life of New York City and other U.S. urban centers. Still to be satisfactorily determined is the extent of the Puerto Rican contribution to salsa, that durable commercial phenomenon of the past three decades, but the opinions of several early participants may be seen in this section, as well as a farewell to one of its most important early practitioners, Rafael Cortijo.

Concert Life

Musical Culture at the Turn of the Century

La Hija del Caribe (Trinidad Padilla de Sanz), "Notas musicales," *Puerto Rico Musical* 1, no. 1 (15 February 1906): 5-6.

The artist is born, not made, as is beyond discussion; however, he will develop and perfect his skills according to the environment in which he finds himself. But without artistic fiber to begin with, he will not have the skills to polish. Puerto Rico is a land of music *par excellence*, whose people possess a fine and delicate ear for music and where with good examples the seed of good taste could bear fruit. However, where this divine art is concerned the island is in its infancy.

The same thing happens in music as in all other branches of knowledge in Puerto Rico; El Caribe[2] was not far from the mark when he wrote "Why must our children, exiled from their homeland, cross the seas in search of knowledge?"

It is not the fault of the noble Puerto Rican people that they are not educated for music's high culture, if those who have crossed the seas to drink at the divine fountains of art do not take the trouble to educate them. No group receives the gift of artistic education through divination: musicians, like painters and writers, are forged and polished in the great centers, workshops of the artistic vision, which reflect the colossal spirit and the incessant hard work of emulation and struggle.

The struggle is arduous in our beautiful garden of Puerto Rico, and let it not be said that it has not produced geniuses. Gonzalo Núñez, that Colossus of Art, could have inspired a great development in the island's musical taste, through teaching and through rooting out the weeds which flourish in our musical garden.[3] However, he has found little field for his aspirations due to Puerto Rico's limited musical horizon, and plans to enrich distant lands with the light of his sovereign genius.

If others do what Núñez has done; if their coldness, their indifference, their lack of love of homeland causes them to view with olympic disdain the poor souls hungry for art's sacrament, why then blame the people of Puerto Rico for their lack of praparation for the high art of music?

Why is it that are we not so backward in literature? Because there is such an institution as the Ateneo, and because there have been men of good will to grasp the golden reins of that temple of knowledge; because in the Ateneo exists emulation, exists controversy: in a word, exists the sacred fire of the vision of patriotism.[4]

With a little patriotism and a little good will, then, it is possible to rise to great heights. But a people does not become educated in the arts by applauding its own dances and its own dance music.[5] It becomes educated through hard work in the arts by those who can contribute directly, through performances of concert music, and through saturating the souls of the people with love for the works of the great masters without wounding their own musical sensibilities, for enduring trees are not created by burning the forests.

1898 and the Change of Government

Fernando Callejo Ferrer, *Música y músicos portorriqueños* (San Juan: Tip. Cantero Fernández & Co., 1915), reprinted as *Música y músicos puertorriqueños,* Amaury Veray, ed. (San Juan: Editorial Coquí, 1971), 67-68.

Consistent with the history of great political upheavals among the peoples of the world, the change of nationality brought the paralysis, if not the regression, of the artistic development whose progress had been so evident in Puerto Rico.

Fortunately, the fundamental changes were hardly noticed in daily life due to the special manner in which the Spanish-American War developed in Puerto Rico, resembling more a peaceful (but armed) visit than a battle.

Not so in the island's official life; the U.S. system of governmental administration was so completely different from the Spanish that it was only natural that the new government should completely uproot the former administrative practices, although most island residents hoped otherwise. The new government then implanted its own methods, both because it considered them better and because history reveals few cases in which a conquering force adopts the ways and customs of the conquered.

It is not the U.S. practice for the State to directly oversee the development of the arts; for this reason one of the first actions of the new regime in Puerto Rico was to terminate all subsidies affecting the arts.

The separation of church and state brought the end of the cathedral orchestra, as well as the end of the post of cathedral organist. The permanent orchestra has never been restored, although the bishopric or the cathedral parish occasionally engages an orchestra for some specific religious observance. As for the organ, the deep, solemn, and mystical harmonies of that noble instrument are hardly heard any more in the majestic naves of our churches.

With the end of scholarships underwritten by the Provincial Delegation, Elisa Tavárez and young Ángel Celestino Morales, beneficiaries of scholarships, were forced to return to the island. Fortunately, they had completed their studies (of piano and violin, respectively) at the Madrid Conservatory.

Convinced that general opinion driven by the spirit of association is what guides (and indeed almost rules) official life in the United States, from the first months of the change of nationality we attempted to unite all of the island's musical forces in a single group as a means toward preventing the decline in the arts which we foresaw. With this in mind, toward the end of December 1898 and supported by such figures as Arteaga, Chavier, Carreras, Pasarell, Cruz, and other valuable Ponce colleagues, we held a public meeting in that city. In that meeting the constitutional bases were approved for the Puerto Rico Musical Association; a local committee was formed, which commissioned Arteaga to carry forward with us the work of organizing the rest of the island.

On December 30 the second formative meeting was held, at the Ateneo in San Juan. Again the constitutional bases were approved and again a local committee was formed; the San Juan committee included Maestro Gutiérrez and the pianist Anita Otero, among others. Gutiérrez was commissioned, together with Arteaga and the present writer, to place in the hands of Governor Henry a document asking him to sponsor the aims of the Association and to underwrite its plan to establish a San Juan Musical Institute.[6] After courteously receiving the commission and learning of our petition through an interpreter, General Henry promised to endorse it favorably to the attention of the head of the Autonomous Cabinet,[7] as indeed he did. However, this official responded negatively, lamenting that he could not honor the nascent association's proposal because his office's limited income barely covered the expenses of his own budget.

In spite of this initial failure our work continued in attempting to definitively constitute an island-wide association, but we eventually had to abandon even this effort. Because of the lack of civic conviction, the character of our musicians was stubbornly opposed to the spirit of affiliation.

The Revival of a Tradition:
Concerts on the Plaza

Editorial: "También los músicos son hijos de Dios," *Puerto Rico Ilustrado* 25, no. 1250 (17 February 1934): 1.

An old custom, which has been passing into memory along with the decline of other worthy aspects of urban culture, will soon be revived thanks to money provided by the PRERA[8] and wisely distributed.

On first sight it might appear as if the funds of this great agency could be put to some more practical use than founding a concert band. However, the truth is that musicians are also God's children, and it is not a bad idea to offer them the means by which in addition to gaining their livelihood, they might provide the city with a touch of art and a cultural expression which our environment has lacked: an environment made wretched by the pressing lack of life's basic necessities. This lack has gradually eliminated the subtle nuances which make life pleasant and bring dignity to a community.

Park band concerts formed part of our old and respected public customs, and one of the successes of the PRERA has been to revive it. On Wednesdays and Sundays music lovers will again have a place to listen to concerts, a pastime which we lost when it became necessary to reduce the budgets of the agencies which supported two excellent ensembles: the Police Band and the Municipal Band.

Under Spanish rule, the regimental bands offered two or three concerts per week, and there was a time when on Thursday and Sunday evenings the main plaza was a meeting place for our most distinguished society. That particular aspect can never be revived, for our tastes and our customs have taken other paths. However, the people, the general population which lacks places of diversion, will have for several months (and we must see that the appropriation continues) an opportunity for entertainment which at the same time can encourage a talent which is widespread among us.

As we have said, the concerts will last some months while the band's expenses are covered by this federal appropriation. However, we must be sure that when this aid runs out, the life of the well organized and functioning band does not also end, having regained the territory lost during the years when we were deprived of this noble diversion.

When the federal appropriation ends, it should not be difficult to organize a voluntary financial effort to keep alive the band to which maestro Miranda[9] has lent his disinterested backing with the generous impulse of one who loves his art and who supports his enthusiasm with his authority and his example. A great number of persons and businesses could be induced to subscribe a monthly sum so that this band, which by then would be functioning smoothly, might live on and develop further with the aid of the residents of San Juan. Because this is an educated community, its residents would certainly not wish to be deprived of the refinements which are so native to it.

It will be necessary to adopt certain measures so that the silence and calm which music requires, not be disturbed by the spontaneous commotion of children who do not use the plaza when it is empty but who flock there when their activities are not appropriate and when the most elemental ideas of culture would advise that they be in their homes. This should be easy. If a few policemen can be stationed in the plaza with the assignment of quelling the games and maintaining silence while the music is playing, in a few weeks the composure which formerly characterized these artistic events can be regained.

Appreciation of music and respect for its performers. How can these virtues not be achieved with the help of artistic temperament and the endorsement of culture?

A Plea for Music in the Schools

Arístides Chavier, "Disquisiciones musicales," *Almanaque puertorriqueño Asenjo 1937* [San Juan: Conrado Asenjo, 1936], 71-72.

Puerto Rican society, and particularly its musical elite, has enjoyed valuable experiences of high art during recent years, revealed by a small group of Puerto Rican artists who have visited us after establishing solid reputations in the principal European and American artistic centers. Such artists, including the Figueroa family[10] and Jesús María Sanromá,[11] have performed a most praiseworthy service, for their admirable skill has revived the interest and enthusiasm which prevailed in times past, when more admiration was expressed for the manifestations of the spirit. Then, the craze for physical sport had not yet enslaved us, nor did it obblige anyone to prostrate himself, quivering in delirious adoration, before the feet of today's hero, the pugilistic conqueror.

But in spite of the brilliant work of these artists, the state of the musical art in today's Puerto Rico is neither attractive nor promising, for in addition to the excessive attention lavished upon physical education, other causes exist which obstruct the development of our musical culture. Among these we may point out the demands of "practical life," as well as brute sensualism and the lack of true love for the higher manifestations of the spirit.

As we lack conservatories and other such institutions in Puerto Rico, I propose the introduction in our schools of the cultivation of music, for it is known that the cultivation of this art is absolutely indispensable for a community's moral progress. It is through music that the individual rises to higher planes of existence; it is through the development of his spirit that he forms a more judicious concept of his own existence and learns to treasure in his soul those exalted virtues which can triumphantly guide him down life's rocky path.

You can be assured that until now, our governments have generally remained indifferent to and unmoved by these truths, and have refused to lend their diligent and efficient cooperation to the development of the musical art. In Europe, and in addition to the conservatories where higher training is received, music teaching is firmly established in the public schools under the direction of able teachers. The beneficial results are obvious.

European and even American cities of equal or lesser importance than San Juan possess sufficient means to contribute to the development of efficient musical organizations. Why then does Puerto Rico, a land of music lovers and a country blessed with musical talent, lack such institutions? Why is musical instruction in the public schools not put right, organizing its study on a rational and methodical basis so that it might bring to the attention of everyone the real and positive importance of such study? Why does the musical art not occupy a favored place among school subjects? Why is it relegated to a position of secondary importance?

Contributing to the present situation are certain firmly rooted prejudices and a false concept inspired by erroneous appreciations of the musical art. Musicians themselves bear some responsibility in this matter, for lacking pondered judgment and with thoughtless levity, they pronounce *urbi et orbi*, like an incontrovertible axiom from some banal music theory text, that music is a "recreational art," expressed through "the combination of sounds in a manner agreeable to the ear." In other words, that music's main purpose is to satisfy a mere physical wish, a selfish pleasure. These well-intentioned but misguided champions of recreation see only one aspect of the situation: the external or self-directed aspect, the only one which can satisfy mediocre minds and those persons who have not had an opportunity to closely examine the other aspect, a function of *esthetic emotion and intellectual enjoyment, abstract and completely unselfish.*

To proclaim that music is a "recreational art," an art of "combinations pleasing to the ear" is to characterize it as a frivolous and insubstantial art, lacking any serious and transcendental meaning. Of course a "physical pleasure" exists, produced by the sonoral effects, and perhaps most of the musical works published today are devoted to this purpose as their only goal. But let it be understood that such works are perishable; they are subject to the vagaries of fashions and snobbery. The true work of art, if it is to endure and accomplish its purpose, is not limited to our ear; it must transcend the ear and rise to the highest regions of the spirit, radiating its luminous beams into our minds, enslaving them and saturating them with the magical and mysterious emanations which make us experience the enchantments of a transcendental world.

The musical art, then, is more than what some persons believe it to be; music is a predominant element in life itself, beyond all human speculation. Beethoven the Colossus expressed this, when he said: "Music is a land in which the spirit lives, thinks, and flourishes; philosophy is nothing but a consequence or derivative of music."

A Government-Sponsored
Symphony Orchestra

Alfredo Matilla Jimeno, "La Sinfónica y la 'Sinfonieta,'" *El Mundo* (San

Juan), 13 April 1948, reprinted in Alfredo Matilla Jimeno, *De música*, Alfredo Matilla Rivas, ed. (San Juan: Editorial de la Universidad de Puerto Rico, 1992), 142-44.

The Communications Authority recently invited the island legislature to attend a rehearsal of its new symphony orchestra and its other recently created ensemble, somewhat questionably called a symphonette.[12]

Not long ago, after attending a closed rehearsal of the Symphony Orchestra under the serious and competent direction of don Jesús Figueroa, I arrived at the conclusion that the initial phase—the most difficult—had been virtually surmounted. After hearing the orchestra's recent programs I can confirm my previous assessment. We now have a symphony orchestra whose basic qualities could not be more promising. The rest of the journey will depend not only on the performers but also on the constant and continuous effort of all of us.

The program chosen for its debut—an almost private performance—was deliberately simple, but easier to hear than to play. I probably need not point out that my own prejudice against any kind of concession to popular taste would have counseled the exclusion of the shallow and ephemeral *Etincelles* waltz by Waldteufel, but in truth the Symphony Orchestra played it so well that it almost resembled a piece of serious music. The rest of the program was impeccable.

The orchestra's best performance was undoubtedly the *Phèdre* overture by Jules Massenet. The strings admirably brought out all of the lyricism of the main themes with precise dynamic shading, while securely attacking the by no means easy passage-work of this overture: historically, a true "overture" to the impressionist movement in French music. Brass and woodwind were also very secure; the ensemble was magnificent.

The "Allegro alla polacca" of the *Trio Serenata* of Beethoven (in an arrangement by Tovani) and the Hungarian March from *The Damnation of Faust* by Berlioz were also admirably played under the baton of don Jesús Figueroa, whose skill and security are always a guarantee of seriousness.

The field of symphonic music which this new and resplendent institution has opened up is immense, and its study and performance require a determined effort. The foundations of our orchestral edifice are solid construction; the rest is a question of time and patience. What we have now is good, but what awaits us must and will be better yet, if we offer our enthusiasm and our collaboration.

The second half of the semi-public rehearsal presented Rafael Hernández and his orchestra.[13] Rafael Hernández has a very important task
before him: the dignifying of commercial music, which has erroneously
been called "the people's music."[14] Radio, motion pictures, and other
disturbing elements in the service of vulgarity have poisoned the public's
taste. Rafael Hernández has in his hands a certain kind of music, and an
orchestra charged with raising it to the level of acceptance within the
dignity of proper musical life. Between the intolerable tunes now in public fashion and the great musical creations of the human spirit there is an
ample territory populated by ordinary overtures and stylized dance music. Rafael Hernández knows this territory perfectly well; in addition he
obviously has the theatrical sense which is essential for the success of
this kind of music. On the other hand, his skill as a composer and his
vast concepts of rhythm and of musical color lead him to create works of
greater breadth than is usually encountered in such music. For this reason this recent program reached triumphant heights, for it pleased the
musically uninitiated without boring the more demanding among the
audience.

Of the works presented the one which really stood out (aside from
The Beautiful Galatea of Suppé) was Hernández' own *Mosaicos No. 1*,
which gathers together the best known works of this inspired and prolific
composer. His suite for chorus and small orchestra, *El negrito que vivió
un mes*, is a praiseworthy attempt to raise melodies of popular extraction
to symphonic status. This attempt is largely successful both melodically
and rhythmically, especially in *Canción de cuna*. Very pleasant is Hernández' *Danza capricho no. 5*, demonstrating that the composer knows
his instrumental resources very well. Hernández' arrangements of *danzas* by Morel Campos and Tavárez are indeed sonorous, although I personally prefer to hear the original intention of such works as they were
conceived by their composers. On this occasion Rafael Hernández' success was as great as it was undoubtedly deserved.

During this second part of the program the Free Schools of Music
Chorus performed the Halleluja Chorus of Handel's *Messiah* with the
"Sinfonieta," under the impeccable direction of Bartolomé Bover. I must
confess that I anticipated this performance with fear, because of the
enormous difficulties which the work entails. But as the performance
developed this fear turned to pleasure, for orchestra, chorus and conductor were truly magnificent; they attained the highest point of the concert,
and evoked a long and richly deserved ovation by the public.

In summary, the occasion united in performance a number of splendid elements for the attainment of grand objectives. It convinced the impenitent unbelievers and it encouraged those of us who always believe in the force of good will as a premise for the projection of greater perspectives.

A Twentieth-Century Opera

Samuel B. Cherson, "Estreno plateado de 'El mensajero de plata,'" *El Nuevo Día* (San Juan), 12 October 1986: 83.

Despite the strong opera tradition that has existed in Puerto Rico for well over a century, very few operas have been composed here and there have been even fewer cases of new operas reaching production. In the last century that musical wonder Felipe Gutiérrez y Espinosa (1825-1899) created *Guarionex*, the first Puerto Rican opera and one of the first in America, which according to contemporaneous sources was presented in San Juan around 1855. This work and the same composer's *El bearnés* have unfortunately been lost, while his third known opera, *Macías*, was produced only in 1977, following the manuscript's discovery in Madrid. As far as the present century is concerned, Amaury Veray is known to have been working on an opera entitled *La danza de Juan Aquilano*, still awaiting completion, while Ignacio Morales Nieva has composed several operas during his residence in Puerto Rico, none of which has seen the light of day. The production of new zarzuelas and operettas has been more abundant.

For these reasons the premiere performance of *El mensajero de plata*, taking place on Thursday evening[15] in the Drama Hall of the Performing Arts Center, bore the signs of an historically important musical accomplishment, and the result met the standards of such events.

El mensajero de plata resulted from a commission extended by the Ópera de Cámara company, thanks to aid provided by the National Endowment for the Arts, Opera for the 80s and Beyond, and local public and private sponsors. Ópera de Cámara operates under the general artistic direction of Luis Pereira, who wisely placed the project in the hands of a talented Puerto Rican team headed by composer Roberto Sierra, librettist Myrna Casas, stage director Pablo Cabrera, designer Jaime Suárez, choreographer Eddie Vázquez and ceramist Lorraine de Castro. On stage was a cast of Puerto Rican singers, while in the orchestra pit was the Continuum ensemble of New York, with Joel Sachs as the production's musical director. In addition, eminent theater consultant María

Irene Fornés came from New York several times to advise on certain
details of the production as it developed.

The subject of *El mensajero de plata* is rooted in regionalist literature, for it deals with the popular annual Fiesta of Santiago Apóstol[16] as
it is celebrated in the island town of Loíza. But contrary to what you
might imagine, the creative focus is anything but folkish. The music is
not rich in *bombas* and *plenas*, nor is the set full of palm trees or of the
familiar refreshment stands and gambling booths of patron saint festivities. Also absent are colorful processions honoring saints, while the
customary brilliance of the raiment of the traditional *vejigantes* and
caballeros[17] is remembered only in a few short dance scenes. Finally, the
libretto draws upon none of the widely known stories dealing with the
Fiesta of Santiago Apóstol. Obviously, an attempt was made to avoid the
attraction of a facile and populist realism, instead pointing in the opposite direction, toward stylization and abstraction. Even so, *El mensajero de plata* remains an undeniably Puerto Rican work.

This stylization of essential Puerto Rican musical values is masterfully attained in Roberto Sierra's successful score. Its musical language
is rooted in the composer's solid European training (Ligeti was his
teacher), evident in the color, phrasing and dissonance treatment of the
instrumental voices—violin, cello, clarinet, horn, trombone, piano, and
percussion—that contribute to this chamber opera which lasts a little
more than an hour. However, the subject has been treated with great
seriousness, without seeking harsh extremes but also without hesitating
to occasionally call upon traditional tonal language, as in the ostinatos
which accompany the narrator. At times there are echoes of the Stravin-
sky of *L'histoire du soldat* or *Petrushka*, and going even farther, the ominous deep tones which mark the entrances of the title figure are reminis-
cent of the Mozart of *Don Giovanni*. To this, Sierra has added a truly
Caribbean sense of rhythm, thus confirming in this work the successful
synthesis which has given character to his recent music.

Percussion writing of Afro-Antillean reminiscence underlies the
changes of mood which occur whenever dances and festivals are mentioned. It also provides a strong rhythmic foundation for the ghostly
dance (in which I could swear that I heard a *coquí*[18]) and the invocation
which follows it to open the second act. These provided one of the opera's most successful scenes both musically and visually.

Sierra's instrumental writing respectfully accommodates the vocal
parts, always allowing the melodic lines to prevail while interweaving
brief phrases and elaborations within the proper balance of forces. A

first-act trio and a second-act quintet are *tours de force* of vocal writing. This commission has enabled Sierra to make a major musical statement.

As the basis of this musical work, librettist Myrna Casas has developed a simple tale whose messenger of death (although the word *mensajero* appears only in the title) comes disguised as a silvery *vejigante*; perhaps *El vejigante de plata* would have been a better title. As the dramatic pivot of the work, this figure's elevated style of expression is rich with frequent repetitions, which evoke resonances of Lorca. There are moments when the movement of the plot becomes static, while the end is inconclusive. Still, the poetic elegance of the text is unquestionable.

Jaime Suárez' sets provide a perfect thread of visual counterpoint within the work's abstract and stylized concept. A few totemic structures made of cast-off lumber, fish tails, ropes, pieces of palm, and other natural materials; these enrich the stage as symbolic allusions to the architecture, the flora and the fauna of the Loíza region. And in the climactic scene of the fisherman's death at the hands of the silvery *vejigante*, a violet curtain rises to enfold them, in an imaginative marine metaphor. Yet with all of the sets' atmospheric effectiveness, more variety in the placement of these structural elements would have been recommendable; the changes of placement for the second act were almost imperceptible. More variety could perhaps have been attained by hanging the pieces at different heights for the second act. Fernando Aguilú's lighting maintained the desired atmosphere of mystery and unreality.

This sense of unreality, far removed from any idea of operatic *verismo* but inherent in both music and libretto, is what stage director Cabrera attempted to mold on the stage. To reinforce it he used ceramic masks on the five principal figures (except on the narrator), thus endowing them with impersonal and archetypal qualities. This effect might be open to question; however, according to Cabrera, the use of masks made it possible to symbolically represent persons of dark skin, associated with the Loíza region, while recognizing that masking is itself an important element in the *Fiesta de Santiago Apóstol* as it is celebrated there.

The performers—soprano Virginia Gutiérrez (Estrella), mezzo-soprano Carmen Cornier (Mina), tenor Alejandro Vázquez (Chaguín and the narrator), baritone Ángelo Cruz (Jacobo), and bass Daniel Bonilla (the silvery *vejigante*—handled their by no means easy vocal and dramatic tasks with complete professionalism. It was not always easy to understand the Spanish, a situation more acute in the women than in the men, but then this is a general problem in opera regardless of the language used. In addition, I frequently sensed a lapse of sustained pitch in the mezzo, affected as this voice was by an intense vibrato.

The instrumentalists displayed great skill with this new music under the direction of Joel Sachs, himself vastly experienced in the music of our time. They were major contributors to this sterling silver premiere, which signals a new and promising era for opera composition in Puerto Rico.

The Avant Garde

Francis Schwartz, "Grupo Fluxus de Puerto Rico." From a presentation before the Círculo Musical Gullaume de Machaut, Guaynabo, Puerto Rico, January 10, 1990.

Grupo Fluxus de Puerto Rico was founded by composers Rafael Aponte-Ledée and Francis Schwartz in 1968 in order to encourage the study and performance of contemporary music in Puerto Rico and the Antilles. In addition to presenting works from the existing modern repertory the group undertook a number of experimental projects in the field of mixed media. This enterprise in advanced concepts contrasted notably with the stylistically conservative musical atmosphere then prevailing in Puerto Rico.

Grupo Fluxus' inaugural concert, taking place in the Ateneo Puertorriqueño on March 8, 1968, called upon the participation of soprano María Esther Robles, dancer and choreographer Carmen Biascoechea and composers Schwartz and Aponte-Ledée. Works of Cage, Xenakis, Etkin, Paraskavaidis, and Aponte-Ledée were presented, in addition to a collective improvisation by Grupo Fluxus. *Auschwitz* by Francis Schwartz was given its premiere performance during this concert, temporarily imprisoning the public while utilizing dance, electronically produced sounds, aromas, projections, and temperature changes within the theater. This was the first time that such a work had been experienced in Puerto Rico.

Between 1968 and 1973 Grupo Fluxus de Puerto Rico presented concerts and lectures devoted to contemporary music in Puerto Rico and the Dominican Republic, with events in Ghent and Paris in 1972. The organization also sponsored public forums and televised debates dealing with the deep conservatism of Puerto Rico's official musical agencies. These included the governmental Puerto Rico Casals Festival, an agency founded in 1956 but which for twenty years did not program works by island composers. Among works receiving their Puerto Rico premiere performances by Grupo Fluxus de Puerto Rico were *Octandre* and *Density 21.5* (Edgar Varèse), *Three Haiku* (Kazuo Fukashima), *Brindis III* and *Brindis IV* (Eduardo Kusnir), *Las Holas* (Juan Hidalgo), *Five Variations for Piano* (Luciano Berio), *Available Forms I* and *December 1952* (Earle Brown), and *A Flower, The Marvelous Widow of Eighteen Springs*, and *4'33"* (John Cage). World premieres included *Quinteto* (Natalio Galán), *Volúmenes* (Rafael Aponte-Ledée), *Auschwitz* and *Cronolumen* (Francis Schwartz), and *Subliminal I* (Graciela Paraskavaidis). Grupo Fluxus' activities with university groups inspired the creation of the student ensemble Soprodimus at the Music Department of the University of Puerto Rico. Aponte-Ledée and Schwartz, then department chairman, were the group's faculty advisors. These activities coincided with the creation within that academic department of the island's first electronic music laboratory.

During its five years of activity, Grupo Fluxus created an awareness of the necessity of providing the Puerto Rican public with access to the musical currents of the twentieth century. Although its existence ended in 1973, its influence on a new generation of Puerto Rican musicians and composers was considerable. This first manifestation of the musical avant garde in Puerto Rico gave way in 1974 to the Puerto Rican Society for Contemporary Music, among whose first directors were composers Schwartz and Aponte-Ledée.

The Puerto Rico Casals Festival: Views and Controversies

Early Hopes and High Ideals

Rafael Montañez, "El significado del Festival Casals," *Artes y Letras* (San Juan), May 1957: 3-4.

In 1939 Prades was a tiny village of barely 5,000 inhabitants, practically unknown even to the French outside of the province of Roussillon, where the Catalonian Pyrenees thrust themselves into French skies. "Prades" meant nothing to the traveler who crossed the region to reach the splendors of the Costa Brava or to the pilgrim in search of the miracles of health which it was said were to be found in its hot springs. In the same region are to be found such names as Lourdes, Aix-les-Termes, Banyuls, Cauterets, Perpignan, Amelie . . . Collioure. . . .

It was here that an illustrious exile from his beloved Catalonia found refuge in the little village of Prades, to live the daily life of the outcast, firm in his concept of freedom and human rights, as long as his ideal of seeing his country freed of the regime which governed it remained un-fulfilled.[19] On settling in Prades, next to the foothills of the lofty and fabled Catalonian peak of the Canigó, Casals vowed to silence his cello to the world; through this means he gives form to the vigor of his spiritual greatness and the shape of his genius, while his homeland suffers the yoke of dictatorship. But the world of art, if not that of politics, was not reconciled to losing him, and after ten years another musician was inspired to add his voice to those of other eminent artists but with more success than they had had, in convincing the exile Casals that the world should not be deprived of the treasure of his living art.

The bicentennial anniversary of the death of Johann Sebastian Bach in July 1950 and the homage which the world was preparing to pay to this supreme genius provided the catalytic impulse that moderated Casals' iron determination. Yes, Casals would preside over a celebration to honor the memory of the greatest musician of all times, but it would have to take place in the tiny and forgotten village of Prades. *Prades*: from that moment its name became known throughout the world. Pablo Casals would again play the cello, and around him would congregate a handful of the world's musical celebrities to join him in paying homage to the great Johann Sebastian Bach.[20]

As if over the village were projected the magic of another biblical star, the caravans flowed toward Prades, but now not carrying those seeking the sulphurous fumes of the village springs or the luminous beaches of the Mediterranean midday. These travelers were headed for the secluded sanctuary of the Church of St. Peter in Prades to anoint themselves in the mystical incense of the music of the Cantor of the Thomaskirche of Leipzig, music born again in this humble French village.

During the following five years the annual Prades Festival has become one of the greatest events in the annals of today's music. Casals' love for his native Catalonia, just across the Spanish border, has made Prades famous. Another of Casals' loves, which his mother instilled in him while he was still in his cradle, is the nostalgic love for her birthplace which she carried like an arrow of yearning and affliction in the heart of a Puerto Rican exile.[21] It is this love which has brought Casals to Puerto Rico to repeat here the miracle of Prades.

In proof of this love, Maestro Casals has decided to make of Puerto Rico his permanent home for this last phase of his incomparable life.

Here he will translate his veneration for his mother into a labor of love devoted to the spiritual and artistic enhancement of the island "so enchantingly beautiful, affectionate, and solicitous where she was born." This decision of Casals' will have consequences whose extent it is not now possible to estimate. The effect on our talented youth began to be felt at the very moment of his arrival. Scholarships were created in Casals' name, enabling gifted students to pursue advanced studies abroad. Seriously being debated at present is the need of establishing centers of basic and higher studies to guide the exceptional musical potential of our people. The imperative urgency of planning the creation of symphony orchestras and choral ensembles has been pointed out. Also pointed out has been the need to deeply explore our folklore in order to create music which will securely define the profile of our personality.

Pablo Casals wants more. He wants to collaborate in that enthusiastic impulse with which Puerto Rico struggles for its prosperity in several fields of human endeavor. He is delighted by Puerto Rico's success in gaining an honored place among the countries of our hemisphere which sustain and daily live the doctrines of liberty for which he has been a martyr.

The reaffirmation of this ideal is emphasized by the celebration of the Casals Festival: to say "Casals" is to say greatness and liberty. The meaning of this festival in the eyes of the rest of the world can be summed up in the words of Carleton Smith, director of the National Arts Foundation of the United States, who arrived in Puerto Rico two weeks ago with the charge of informing Casals that the organization which he heads intends to establish five grand awards, equivalent to the Nobel Prizes. These will be conferred upon persons who render extraordinary service to humanity in fields of the arts and sciences. Referring to Puerto Rico's privilege in being the seat of the Casals Festival, the distinguished visitor has said that in his opinion this festival will be the most outstanding cultural event in the history of the Western Hemisphere. I firmly believe that there is no exaggeration in his words.

1957: The Inaugural Concert

Alfredo Matilla Jimeno, "Concierto Inaugural: El Mejor Tributo a Casals," *El Mundo* (San Juan), 24 April 1957: 5, reprinted in Matilla Jimeno, *De Música*, 533-34.

A quiet tension was in the air as the Festival Orchestra began the overture to the *First Suite* of Bach. We all missed the presence of Mae-stro Casals.[22] The magic of his art and the irresistible power of his per-sonality are irreplaceable, and the void which his illness has caused us could only be filled by our emotion. And it was the musicians' emotion, joined to that of the audience, which made of that unforgettable evening a perfect tribute to the one who had made possible such abundant gran-deur without being able to fulfill his inspired purpose himself. The best remembrance and the best token of respect would be to perform well the music over which he would have presided. On his sickbed Pablo Casals could read the sincere reverence of the message which the artists were composing in letters of the heart in this magnificent inaugural concert.

Alexander Schneider has prepared an exceptional orchestra, and there will be much to say in general gratitude about his heroic labor and painstaking attention. All of the orchestra members are admirable per-formers, and with this orchestra all is possible. What an orchestra Casals would have had! This is the finest of all of the instrumental ensembles which have formed his chain of festivals. Schneider has placed all of his heart and his talent at the service of the excellent musicality of the mem-bers, who follow his conducting with impressive security and under-standing. The result was a great concert, a superb concert, a sumptuous concert worthy of any city in the world.

The sum total of all of these glories gives us an idea of the signifi-cance of this festival inauguration for all of us. And above all, an idea of what each performer carried in his heart in order to do what Maestro Casals wished to accomplish so that Puerto Rico might feel proud. In this way has begun a tribute of admiration and affection to one who mer-its it more than anyone else. And in this way the door to emotion has been opened: to the best of emotions, which is born of the ability to wit-ness that which history—the world's tribunal—will remember among the great triumphs of the human spirit.[23]

A Divergent Opinion

Rafael Aponte-Ledée, "Casals: un agente para la penetración cultural," *Música* (Havana), no. 28 (1972): 5-7.[24]

In 1956, by decree of the transitory governor of the Commonwealth of Puerto Rico, legislation created a monopolistic agency which would become still another point of foreign cultural penetration within Puerto Rico's artistic world: the Casals Festival Corporation.

A year later, in 1957, the dazzling promise of the new imperialistic agency was a reality, as the first Puerto Rico Casals Festival took place. Through amendments to the original law, the Casals Corporation was authorized in 1959 to increase its field of activity through the creation and management of a subordinate agency appropriate for the dissemination of symphonic music. The present Puerto Rico Symphony Orchestra came into being in this way. Within a short time and with its budget increased by a Ford Foundation grant of $375,000, the orchestra expanded its field of activity while spreading a false image of Puerto Rico as a prosperous country, a model of progress and felicity thanks to its special condition as a protegé of the United States, through lightning tours of neighboring Caribbean and Central American countries.[25]

In this way, Casals Festival Inc. began to fulfill its role as a precious jewel of the "Showcase of Democracy," a favorite slogan of colonial administrators in referring to our country. The Puerto Rico Conservatory of Music was inaugurated in 1960, as a crowning symbol for the Casals Festival Corporation, which itself had resulted from an initiative rooted in tourism. And in a recent proposal, the managers of the Casals enter-prises have asked of the stateless government of Puerto Rico, additional legislation which would allow them to control all appropriations for cultural purposes which might be made by the government of Mister Ferré.[26] In this ominous document are outlined the ambitious plans for control over theater, ballet and opera which would finally consolidate the monopolistic consortium of Casals Festival Inc.

Ever since the foreboding day of it creation, Casals Festival Inc. has distinguished itself by faithfully fulfilling its alienating mission as it marginalizes our finest performers and composers, applying procedures both subtle and daring.

The music of our composers has been condemned to ostracism, while some excellent Puerto Rican musicians have been displaced or openly marginalized.[27] On the other hand, others have been contracted in order to mask what is widely known by all cultural workers whose attitude before the suffocation of daily life is honest and progressive, despite the habitual deformations of the mass communications media and the repul-sive posture of the traitor. A few Puerto Rican musicians are contracted, then tamed and used as a spearhead against their colleagues; they become a smokescreen in the sterile effort to disguise the Corporation's vast ruthlessness. Naturally, the intimidation of Puerto Rican performers who are faculty members of the Conservatory of Music is the order of the day. This cynical repression—which also extends to compatriots who are members of the Puerto Rico Symphony Orchestra—is evident in the contracts which must be signed very shortly before the beginning of the orchestra season or the academic year as well as in their salaries, which are considerably lower than those received by their foreign colleagues. In addition, no collective bargaining agreement exists for the musical workers in the Casals Festival Inc. enterprises; they are forced to accept a prefabricated contract which permits no discussion.

It is no accident that Mister Pablo Casals is an employee of the executive branch of the colonial government. The agency which bears his name is a subsidiary of the Puerto Rico Industrial Development Company, the intermediary in everything connected with the establishment in Puerto Rico of foreign industrial enterprises.[28] And within this framework of service to absentee capitalism, the Casals myth fulfills its role in the creation of a "favorable industrial climate." While the capitalists order the razing of entire towns, they find it convenient for their purposes to hide the corpses and the misery. In this aspect the old man becomes a profitable investment. Casals becomes a screen to hide the abuse and the infamy; flocks of tourists invade our island to consume the picturesque product called Casals, bringing with them bountiful profits for the tourist industry.

These conditions, so favorable to Rockefeller, IBEC, Sears, and Ford, could never be attained in a country conscious of its history, its culture, and its traditions. Therefore, imperialism uses the Casals agency to subtly persecute, marginalize, and neutralize our musicians, thus disparaging our art as part of the empire's intention to divide us.

A Composer Speaks

"Un festival que se llama Casals." An interview with Francis Schwartz, *Avance* (San Juan) 1, no. 46 (4 June 1973): 12-13.[29]

Avance: First of all, we'd like you to tell us how you see the role of the Puerto Rico Casals Festival in the island's musical life.

Schwartz: Casals Festival, Inc. is the most powerful agency presently engaged in music here, and the one with the biggest budget. But in order to provide an adequate picture of the organization's impact on Puerto Rico's cultural life we must place it in perspective, for it really represents three different but related agencies. These are the Puerto Rico Conservatory of Music, the Puerto Rico Symphony Orchestra and the summer concert series or festival.[30]

First, let's talk about the summer festival, the two weeks of concerts which are presented annually in the University of Puerto Rico Theater. Internationally renowned performers have regularly presented a high level of music in these concerts. However, over the years I have pointed out that a faulty pedagogical concept has led the festival management into what is described as a chronological kind of long range concert programming for the Puerto Rican public, beginning with eighteenth century works and very slowly moving forward over the years and decades. In the meantime this has left the programming bereft of the works of the most highly regarded contemporary composers worldwide. And it is this factor which has made the summer festivals extremely conservative: completely divorced from the currents of today's music. In other words, it's been pedagogically wrong from the start. This attitude seems to be changing a bit now, and we're beginning to see some works by composers of this century. But I think we're far from the time when we will enjoy avant-garde music on this series.

On the other hand, and reflecting a situation which I have described on several occasions, the summer festival has never programmed a work by a Puerto Rican composer or one resident here. I have always maintained that the festival is obliged to present good compositions by island composers, and there certainly are some good works and able island composers. In addition to encouraging the art of composition in Puerto Rico, this practice would acquaint the excellent visiting festival artists with our music, which would aid in its dissemination abroad. And finally, it would be a matter of pride for Puerto Rico, for it would constitute recognition of the island's artistic production as performed by noted artists.[31]

I must point out, however, that the summer festival is not the most important component of Casals Festival, Inc. It is an attractive concert series providing two weeks of concentrated musical activity, certainly, but it can never affect Puerto Rico's own musical life as profoundly as do the Puerto Rico Symphony Orchestra and the Puerto Rico Conservatory of Music.

Avance: How, then, do you see the Casals Festival organization in terms of the summer concerts?

Schwartz: The summer concerts are a point of contact, a link between Puerto Rico and the greater world of international music-making. But as I said earlier, I insist that the summer festival must seek ways to integrate itself into Puerto Rico's own musical life. And that could only be done by incorporating local musical production into the summer festival.

Avance: Then you believe that the really fundamental elements of the festival organization for music in Puerto Rico, are the Puerto Rico Conservatory of Music and the Puerto Rico Symphony Orchestra?

Schwartz: Definitely. The Conservatory of Music produces performers as well as some music teachers for the schools, and the Symphony Orchestra takes concert music to the farthest corners of the island, integrating its music into the daily life of the people. The contribution of the Conservatory in the production of performers has been great. For that reason it is important that it continue improving its curriculum in order to produce more and better performers. The Symphony Orchestra is extremely important because it represents the continuing education of the people, and that is what in the long run will have an effect on the island's culture.

Pablo Casals in Puerto Rico:
An Overview and a Conclusion

Donald Thompson, "Pablo Casals (1876-1973)," in *Encuentro. Cien años de convivencia: España y Puerto Rico*. Exposition Catalogue, Santillana del Mar, Spain and San Juan, Puerto Rico, 1994 (San Juan: Universidad Interamericana de Puerto Rico, 1994), 98-101.

One of Casals' students in Prades was young Marta Montañez, a promising cellist and a member of a musical Puerto Rican family.[32] This fact, added to Casals' desire to visit his mother's birthplace, a desire often expressed but never realized, motivated him to finally visit Puerto Rico.[33] This visit, taking place from December 1955 to March 1956, was followed by two events of the greatest importance in the life of Pablo Casals: his marriage to his student Marta Montañez and the establishing of his home in Puerto Rico. Beginning in 1957, San Juan would serve as the hub of a new series of musical endeavors undertaken by Casals: endeavors to which he would devote the rest of his long life with characteristic energy and dedication.

In addition, this visit prepared the ground for the creation of new musical institutions and new cultural initiatives in Puerto Rico. In 1957 a series of annual musical festivals was launched in Puerto Rico, a series based on the presence of the admired cellist himself and organized by his devoted colleague, violinist Alexander Schneider. The Puerto Rico Casals Festivals were originally sponsored by a group of the cellist's admirers in Puerto Rico, but soon inspired the creation of a government branch specifically charged with their management. Held on the campus of the University of Puerto Rico, a charming location of great cultural significance, the early festivals evoked the companionship, the emotion, and the musical brilliance of the Prades festivals themselves. In addition, they provided an important factor in the flow of visitors to the island, a subject of great interest to the insular government and especially to its tourism and industrial development branches.

A second consequence of Casals' presence in Puerto Rico was the creation of an official conservatory of music. The present Puerto Rico Conservatory of Music was established in 1959 as a subsidiary of the Puerto Rico Casals Festival Corporation. A third result of this powerful musical presence in Puerto Rico was the creation of a new Puerto Rico Symphony Orchestra, which would offer its first concerts in 1958.

As is the case of musical instruction in Puerto Rico, the island's orchestral tradition has roots which go back to the early nineteenth century. During the past century and longer, Puerto Rico has had a population of able instrumentalists available for concerts, for duty in the theater orchestra pit, and for the formation of chamber ensembles, but the island has not always been blessed with stable sponsoring institutions. Concert orchestras existed, with such titles as "Puerto Rico Symphony Orchestra" and "Puerto Rico Philharmonic Orchestra," but their existence was precarious, unstable, and generally short.[34]

The present Puerto Rico Symphony Orchestra, then a new subsidiary of the Puerto Rico Casals Festival Corporation, offered its first concerts in 1958. As a powerful emotional and symbolic note, the orchestra's inaugural concert took place under Casals' direction in Mayagüez, his mother's birthplace. Originally, the new orchestra's program was mainly limited to light music, with its concerts offered in town plazas and other places of easy public access, with free admission.

Those first seasons, of barely three weeks' duration, have grown greatly during the orchestra's almost four decades of existence. Its recent seasons have been forty weeks and more in length, with a fully symphonic repertory and with a significant proportion of internationally known conductors and soloists. Since 1981 the Puerto Rico Symphony Orchestra has been the resident orchestra of the Puerto Rico Casals Festival, which is still observed annually.

Under governmental auspices and as the direct descendant of that short-lived ensemble which offered open-air concerts in November 1958, the Puerto Rico Symphony Orchestra has become the anchor of Puerto Rico's musical life. It represents Pablo Casals' most fundamental, most vital, and most solid legacy in Puerto Rico.

Pablo Casals died in San Juan, Puerto Rico, on October 22, 1973. The following day, the Puerto Rico Symphony Orchestra played the funeral march from Beethoven's *Eroica Symphony* before his coffin, on view in the Capitol Building of the Commonwealth of Puerto Rico. This was an exquisitely appropriate farewell gesture, offered by the orchestra whose inaugural concert Casals had conducted fifteen years before: the orchestra which today constitutes a living monument and Casals' most significant legacy to the Caribbean island where his mother had been born almost a century and a half before.

Urban Popular and Commercial Music

The Songs of Rafael Hernández

Margot Arce, "Puerto Rico en las canciones de Rafael Hernández," *Isla* (San Juan) 1, no. 4 (December 1939): 4-6.[35]

A rigorous classification of the music and the texts of Rafael Hernández' songs would first require us to establish a clear distinction between "popular" and "folk" expression. In folk art, the culture and the sentiments of an entire people are manifested as a spontaneous life force unconscious of itself; the anonymous creator becomes simply the spokesman for the transmission of collective perceptions and collective aspirations. As the poet Yeats would say, folklore is usually "the impassioned expression of rare and delicate intuitions." For this reason we often encounter and admire examples of folk art that have attained poetic or artistic beauty which would be difficult to surpass.

In what we call popular art, in order to distinguish it from folk art (as the two terms are often treated as synonyms), an identifiable artist creates an art work, but always having folk art in mind and consciously stylizing his work in a form which will approach the spontaneity of the people. In other words, that which among the people is born and flows naturally, is deliberately cultivated by the artist. At times, the artist accomplishes a perfect union with the collective spirit of the folk. Then the people themselves adopt the work, claiming it as their own, and transmit it as they would a work of their own creation, as folk art.

Menéndez Pidal, speaking of Spanish poetry, cites cases in which works of recognized poets have been adopted by the folk, who then modify them and treat them as their own. Other historians of folklore have denied the existence of a true folk origin of art, believing that "folk art" originates in the imitation of high art, with the product then forming part of a folk tradition.

The songs of Rafael Hernández belong to the type of art which we have described as popular. Hernández knows music and poetry and has undertaken technical studies in music. However, when composing he imitates (as he himself has expressed it), attempting to capture the spirit of the island's folk song. That he has succeeded in attaining this perfect union is confirmed by the wide and rapid diffusion of his songs and the popularity which they have attained from the beginning. And if the historians referred to above were correct in affirming that only a "popular" tradition really exists among the folk, we may be witnessing a process of transformation as the songs of Rafael Hernández become converted into folk music. By this I mean that as time passes it would not be strange if these songs were to form part of the collective heritage of folklore. Some of his songs have in fact attained that desired state.

Rafael Hernández writes several kinds of songs: songs with Puerto Rican themes, songs of nature, songs of love, and songs of pain. And in all of them he speaks of his people or for his people. At times he speaks to us of his sentiments and his personal views concerning Puerto Rico, or of its countryside, or of its problems; at other times he transmits a collective spirit as he sings of his love of Puerto Rico or of the island's natural beauty. In the first case he speaks for himself; in the second he is a loyal spokesman. This is the secret of the success of his songs; Puerto Rico finds in them the voice of its own heart, and sees itself in them as in a mirror.

Rafael Hernández loves his homeland. Long years abroad, filled with undertakings in distant lands, have not stilled his memories of childhood in Aguadilla, nor the sentimental echoes of island melodies, nor the images of our placid landscapes. During twenty years in New York he refuses to succumb to the foreign environment, and so can criticize those compatriots who so easily and so frivolously adopt the foreign plumage. He stands firmly behind his defenses, and continues steadfast in his adherence to his homeland and its traditions. Nor does he permit jazz rhythms or the Cuban rumba to adulterate the Puerto Rican flavor of his music. He wants modern Puerto Rican music to retain the true flavor of the island and to express the truth of our souls.

The example of Rafael Hernández merits emulation, and we need his example at this moment. We all suffer from the vice of overestimating the value of everything which comes from abroad, while deprecating through snobbery and pedantry the very little which still remains of our own culture. We are not conscious of how grotesque the result of this substitution is, nor do we realize that we are headed toward cultural suicide. Some voices have been raised in alarm, but unfortunately they are preaching in the desert. Rafael Hernández, far from Puerto Rico and in a constant battle with life's daily demands, has done much more than he realizes for the preservation of our culture. And in many cases his work has been more effective than that of the intellectuals. His love of his homeland and his singing of sentiments which still live in our hearts in spite of everything, establish a subtle form of communication among all Puerto Ricans. As we sing them a true common denominator moves within us, albeit unconsciously, and we find ourselves united in the very roots of sentiment. All of Puerto Rico's social classes, including city dwellers and country folk, the illiterate and the educated, the young and the old, at some moment find solace in the evocative and tender melodies of "Capullito de alelí," "Tú no comprendes," "La casita," "Traición." In moments of intimacy, when we permit the heart to express its deepest truths, and when intellectual pride fails to render us cold and dry, the songs of Rafael Hernández again unite us in that romantic melancholy, warm and vibrant, which is our usual spiritual state. Then we confront the simplest of realities, the human and eternal realities which an intellectualizing century has not been able nor will ever be able to erase.

The songs of Rafael Hernández based on Puerto Rican themes are divided into three groups: songs that praise the beauty of this land, songs of social and patriotic theme, and songs that express the sentiments of the people.

Hernández' vision of nature results from the nostalgia which in turn stems from his memories of the island. The poet in him speaks of warm and starlit nights, of blue skies, radiant sun, the singing of birds, the fragrant and humid earth. Emotion drives him to hyperbole, to terms of delight and tenderness. Enchantment and glorification are the fundamental tones; Hernández sings like a lover. For example, remember the melody and the words of "Los carreteros." In other songs Hernández describes the earth; in "Los carreteros" he is the instrument of the earth itself, its own unmistakable voice. All of the mild and melancholy enchantment of the Puerto Rican daybreak, the vegetation's perfume, the *coquí's* piercing call, the languor of awakening, the comely and voluptuous illusion of a tropical sunrise: all vibrate in the melody and the rhythm of "Los carreteros." We hear the song and hear our own blood singing; we feel our own roots penetrating this earth, for there is the ultimate lifeblood of our existence.

In his patriotic songs and those dealing with social themes, Hernández' lyricism becomes transformed into drama. The poet is moved by a yearning for liberty and, on the other hand, by the tragedy surrounding him. "Lamento borincano," with the unity and accuracy of literary legend, consolidates the entire history of our disillusionment. The *jibarito,* who like the legendary milkmaid goes to market full of hope but returns defeated, her hopes shattered, is the most glowing symbol of our social and political life. Between the lines of the song the poet reveals his protest, his cry of rebellion, his passion for justice; sentiments which he will again express in other songs: "Pobre Borinquen," "Si tengo razón," "El buen borincano," "Libertad," "Preciosa." "Lamento borincano" is the true hymn of our people, the elegy of its failure and of its desperation. A North American, Earl Hanson, has expressed this vision in the title of a famous article of his. In "Lament for Puerto Rico," Hanson with prodigious indignation protests the way his compatriots have treated their Caribbean colony. Rafael Hernández, also touched by his *jíbaro's* desolation, ends by declaring in another song that although all of the other lands of America have attained their liberty by the manly effort of their sons, "Only God will give it" to our island. Hernández can now only hope for a miracle to occur.

We have said that Hernández' sentimental songs express the feelings of our people: their attitudes toward love and the problems it creates. In his songs echo our diluted romanticism, our sensuality, our passion, with our melancholy occasionally relieved by a note of bitter or cheerful humor. Hernandez' lyrics reflect the popular speech of Puerto Rico: slow of rhythm, full of exaggerated qualifiers, sentimental, rich in diminutives and other affectionate expressions. This speech is marvelously adapted to Hernández' repetitive rhythms and to the ingenious lyricism of his widely varied melodies.

What is surprising about these songs, so much our own, is the popularity which they have earned throughout Hispanic America. Rafael Hernández, while expressing the sentiments of Puerto Ricans, has touched the most secret vein of the Hispanic heart: a vein which is not the exclusive inheritence of any specific country or climate, but which unites us all through the mysterious bond of blood. The heart of all of Spanish America sings with Rafael Hernández.

"Jibaro" Dances

Miguel Meléndez Muñoz, "Los 'bailes jíbaros,'" in his *Obras completas*, 3 vols. (Barcelona: Ediciones Rumbos, 1963), 3, 750-55.

Many parties are held and many festive occasions are observed in Puerto Rico during the last months of the waning year. Some events are of religious nature while others are of deep and living tradition: the Discovery of Puerto Rico, for example, or *Thanksgiving Day*,[36] although the year might have brought us nothing for which to be thankful. Many of these activities take place in November.

But also taking place in November and December are other secular festivities, indeed too secular—offensive, in fact—because of their deceit, because of their traditional banality, and because of the failure of their purpose. I am speaking of "jíbaro" dances as they are organized by Puerto Rican society.

Bailes jíbaros are staged—the correct word, I assure you—in urban casinos,[37] social clubs, and other such establishments during the Christmas season and until Three Kings Day in January. I say "staged," because they are deliberately mounted with all of the childish and irresponsible theatricality of a fool. And furthermore, they fail to attain even a parodic purpose because of the time of year at which they are organized; it would be much more "reasonable" (within their complete lack of reason) to offer them as masquerade balls or street parties during Carnival, thus adding to the traditional tumult and disorder of that event.

Out of curiosity I have attended some of these dances in recent years. And when the participants' noisy delight and their expressions of exhilaration reach their highest point I have felt out of place, perplexed and depressed, as if I were witnessing for the first time some rare spectacle taking place in some nonexistent land: a spectacle of extravagant invention. And for that reason the land which could actually enjoy such a spectacle did not exist either.

Anyone who has attended real dances in the real countryside can only wonder what kind of dances these are and what kind of country people they represent? Neither the costumes which the dancers adopt nor the physical attitudes which these pseudo-*jíbaros* affect has anything to do with the reality, which in any case has faded into the past.

Who has seen today's Puerto Rican rural laborer (or yesterday's, for that matter) dancing inside a house, however poor and humble, with his hat pulled down to his ears? When has he used brightly colored handkerchiefs around his neck in the fashion of neckties?

Anyone who knows the life and customs of our country people knows that they have never had a characteristic form of dress. The Spanish tradition, so rich and varied in the arts of colorful dress and decoration, was never transplanted whole to our island. Aside from matters of climate and of the regional origin in Spain of those who colonized and populated Puerto Rico in the first phase of Spanish domination, our rural laborers have never dressed in even a simple imitation of the dress which was used and which is still observed in many regions of Spain.

Many, many years ago I took a friend from San Juan on an excursion to the country. He had never been beyond Río Piedras and had a very vague and very conventional idea of the Puerto Rican countryside. My plan was to treat him to everything which at that time was expected of such excursions: a trip to the mountains, a lunch of the inevitable roast pork with white rice, etc., etc. And even a dance, which although featuring authentic and pretty country girls would, I knew, display nothing of the conventionally accepted *jíbaro* style, neither the dance nor the girls themselves.

When we arrived at the house which had been prepared for the party, my friend asked, "But . . . this is a *jíbaro* dance? Look at the *girls*,[38] with those dresses of the latest fashion, their hair permed, nylon stockings, complete makeup, secure and open. . . ." "And brazen, like those of our great cities and towns," I interrupted. "Where are the *jibaritas* with their long flounced dresses of vibrant colors, their sweet bodies tightly girdled, their long tresses, their handkerchiefs, aromatic with herbs, covering their adorable heads, and with their timid behavior? And the *jíbaros* with their great straw hats, their brightly colored sashes, their tremendous cigars producing smoke like chimneys, their long machetes hanging from their waists as in the *bailes jíbaros* of San Juan's casinos, clubs, sororities, ... where are they?" he asked.

I explained to him that physically, the countryside had not changed very much. It is true that deforestation, the unplanned and irrational clearing of the forests, has impoverished us somewhat by taking away the powerful beauty and the cheerfulness of the great trees. All the rest, the human element, is in full and constant evolution: habits, clothing, tastes, enthusiasms, and attitudes concerning life and society. This is the result of progress and of fashion, which always moves right along with it. The stores full of ready-made clothing, manufactured in innumerable patterns; the excessive and outrageous commercial competition; cosmopolitanism, which tends to flatten out and uniformize everything in the way of individual economic capacity in today's social life: all of these factors have precipitated in our country the ancient laws of imitation.

The *jíbaro* you seek is simply not to be found today. The *jíbaro* as preserved in fanciful legends and traditional stories is almost exclusively the product of the many *costumbrista* writers who have tried (in vain) to fix and perpetuate the outlines of the *jíbaro*. In their vision, one must seek out the *jíbaro*, unveil him and treat him with brotherly affection and eager understanding in order to discover his noble, tolerant, and generous soul.

And the good Puerto Rican laborer who sees himself so poorly parodied in those absurd *bailes jíbaros*, can only exclaim, in the timeless style of his ancestors, "¡Ay, compay, no me jaga reil que tengo el labio paltío!"[39]

Salsa: Two Early Views

Manuel Silva Casanova, "¡Salsa!," *Avance* (San Juan) 2, no. 57 (20 August 1973): 10-18.

Whether seen as a step backward in popular music or as a mixture of old Afro-Cuban rhythms or perhaps only as the *bombas* and *guaguancós* of Cortijo in new arrangements of the 70s, salsa music will take its place in history as a cultural phenomenon of our time. Singers, musicians, arrangers, composers of concert music, composers of popular music, musicologists: all are talking about salsa. Puerto Rican and New York newspapers devote entire pages to the "salsa phenomenon." Salsa festivals attract tens of thousands of *salseros* to basketball courts, baseball parks, and sports stadiums, where the most popular bands offer concerts, "operas" and "hand-to-hand" competitions which last twelve or thirteen hours without interruption.

While salsa has experienced the greatest acceptance in the slums, the housing projects and other areas inhabited by the poor and middle classes, the impact of these rhythms (especially the *guaguancó*) has also reached higher economic levels. It is not unusual to find new bands with such names as Revolución, Tentación Latina, Explosión, Conspiración, or Invasión playing in hotel ballrooms where a few years ago only the conventional styles of Lito Peña and César Concepción were tolerated.

As was to be expected, the salsa phenomenon has evoked different reactions from different sectors of the population. Orchestras organize salsa festivals for charitable purposes and such agencies as CREA[40] form their own salsa bands, while a Chicago group offers a salsa concert in the patio of the august Institute of Puerto Rican Culture itself. But at the same time there are those who rail against salsa music. Alfred D. Herger, on assuming his new post as general manager of the "Gran Cadena" station WQBS, almost completely eliminated what he called "strong and strident" music in order to create in radio a "refuge from the salsa invasion."

Tommy Olivencia, the noted trumpet player and bandleader, sees salsa as nothing new:

> Salsa is the music of nine or ten years ago: *guaguancó* and *bomba*. "Salsa" is just a word, and although the arrangements are more modern the music remains the same. For me the "new era" of salsa really goes back to the time when Cortijo made the *bomba* and *plena* famous and later the *guaguancó* and the music of the streets.

Olivencia also sees a dangerous relation between the youth salsa culture and drugs:

> For my part, I wish to point out that the drug problem is going to bring an end to salsa music in Puerto Rico, or at least in San Juan. And though a while ago there was a problem of heroin use by some musicians, now the problem is caused by young *salseros* themselves, who have caused problems at some dances. Not all, but there is a group which sets out to wreck the musical environment. There are hotels in San Juan which will not rent their ballrooms for dances where salsa will be played, fearing the behavior of the *salsero* mob.

How Puerto Rican is Salsa?

Among these reactions and in the light of the growing significance of the subject of salsa, a number of studies have already been directed toward this phenomenon, a phenomenon which has revolutionized Puerto Rican popular music as well as Latin music generally. This becomes important as we realize that no satisfactory explanation has as yet been offered of what this new style of expression represents within our culture. Is salsa Puerto Rican? Is there a new tendency in Puerto Rican popular music or is this merely a repetition of old rhythms in new arrangements? Is it perhaps a claim of cultural identity on the part of the present generation? What really is salsa?

Héctor Campos Parsi, the composer of concert music, believes that there is nothing new in the rhythmic structure of salsa, and sees it rather as a regression in the development of popular music. "It's the same thing as the montuno of the 1940s," says Campos Parsi:

> The difference is in the instrumentation. And as for the proliferation of
> salsa groups, I see nothing out of the ordinary. The same thing happened
> in the United States when audiences tired of the big bands and small rock
> groups began to flourish: the Beatles, the Rolling Stones, etc. However,
> this doesn't mean that I reject salsa music. On the contrary, I consider it
> a genuine manifestation of our cultural concerns, and something which
> a great part of our population deeply enjoys.

Commercialization, a phenomenon which permeates every aspect of
life in contemporary Puerto Rico, has perhaps provided the broadest
definition to the concept: any group which plays the African-derived styles
of *mambo*, *guaguancó*, or *montuno* is now called a salsa band. Salsa has
revolutionized the world of popular music in a great number of ways; we
now have salsa dancers, salsa arrangers, agents seeking salsa talent, salsa
radio stations, and more; however, it is the recording companies which
have taken the lead in the dissemination of these rhythms. With the
"salsa" label, everything sells. For this reason we can find a dozen salsa
bands, all under the same recording company label, offering a stadium
concert before ten or twelve thousand people. Nevertheless, a difference
exists between the salsa band and the conventional dance band, a difference which arose with the incorporation in the new bands of a specific
dominant element: the trombone. It is true that the trombone was used
prior to the appearance of salsa bands, but until now it had never dominated the instrumentation. Willie Colón, one of the pioneers of Puerto Rican
salsa, abandoned the saxophone section entirely, and in recent years his
recordings have maintained first place in public taste both on radio and
in record sales. Other groups which also favor the trombone are Roberto
and his New Montuno, The López Brothers, Tempo 70, and Impacto
Crea. The Gran Combo, a generally conservative group which always
based its wind section on saxes and trumpets, has also included the
trombone in its instrumentation, giving its arrangements a light touch of
salsa.

The Dilemma of a Saxophone Player

Salsa has brought with it a whole series of innovations which have
affected not only the sound and the harmonic structure of popular music,
but also such aspects as the amplification of sound, the musicians' way

of dressing, choreographic routines, bands' names, publicity styles, and group dynamics. Subjects which attract the songwriters are now tied to Puerto Rican identity and the claim of cultural values rather than to the sentimental and politically neutral subjects of the *guaracha* of two decades ago. "I think we're talking too hastily about salsa," says Radamés Sánchez, leader of the Unión Taína Orchestra:

I play saxophone, and I was never so conscious of it as since the arrival on the scene of salsa. It is precisely the rejection of the saxophone and the rise of the trombone which marks the development of salsa. What I'm about to say may seem strange, but every day it's harder to find work as a saxophone player. It's as if the sax, especially the alto and the soprano (lately the baritone has had some demand), had been taken out of the race. The coarse sound of the trombone now takes the lead in salsa arrangements. It's for this reason that salsa bands can't play a delicate bolero.

Radamés believes that the decline of the *agogo* style has been an important factor in the rise of salsa:

The *agogo* musicians realized that they couldn't create anything new; they apparently grew tired of copying musical patterns that they couldn't feel or understand. All of their youthful energy and need of recognition appears to have found a place in salsa, for many of the salsa bass and keyboard players have come from *agogo* groups.

There are many angles of this trend which cannot be ignored, for they are symptomatic of a new social turmoil. Some of these angles tend toward the deterioration of music itself, but in any case they are aspects of the new wave. Many salsa musicians are relatively young. Many can't even express their thoughts concerning a movement which they themselves initiated and which undercuts older patterns. To the older patterns, this new style represented irrelevant protest music, or some way of proclaiming Puerto Rican identity.

Salsa music has introduced many changes in the musical milieu; its arrival has not been marked solely by changes in the style of arrangements or in the rhythmic patterns or harmony. In fact, a whole range of traits characterizes today's salsa music. For example, we hear numbers which proclaim Puerto Rican identity, like "Jíbaro soy" or "Soy boricua;" songs which identify with the poor, such as "Pa' los caseríos," "Tumbaron la Veintiuna," or "De Barrio Obrero a la Quince."

Another very interesting aspect of the Puerto Rican salsa bands is the

introduction of a new style of band names. The word "combo," derived
from "combination," has virtually disappeared. In a curious concordance,
Puerto Rican bands of the salsa era claim such names as Revolución,
Explosión Latina, Revelación, Unión Taína, Conspiración, Tentación, etc.
The new ensembles have gained a greater sense of collective endeavor,
and except in some "upper class" dance orchestras, the cult of the leader
has practically disappeared.

Also noted in the music of these groups—especially that of salsa bands
based in New York—is a certain nostalgia, a yearning to "return," or to
reaffirm Puerto Rican origin. This is evident in such tunes as "Mi jara-
gual" and "Dile que tú eres puertorriqueño." Their identification with this
yearning has brought fame to an orchestra which overnight became a
symbol of salsa. The La Selecta orchestra has had an impact comparable
only to that of the sensational bomba and plena *bembés* of Rafael Cortijo
in the dance halls of New York and Puerto Rico a little more than a decade ago.

According to Rafi Leavit, La Selecta leader,

> The phenomenon is easy to explain. So much emphasis was given to
> American music that Puerto Ricans decided to identify with their own
> music. And you see how popular our latest *décima* tunes have been. Our
> intention with "Jíbaro soy" was to introduce jíbaro music. Why play only
> Cuban tunes? I had two bands before, and I remember that everything we
> played was copied from someone else. But there's no doubt that ever since
> we became involved with real salsa, what has been foremost in our
> arrangements is originality.
>
> And salsa has been a hit on all social levels. Our band has played in
> the exclusive areas of Miramar and the Condado as well as in the poorer
> districts and the housing projects. The rise of salsa coincides with an era
> of coming together of certain sectors of the population. This reaffirmation
> of our cultural traits advances the cause of salsa music as something truly
> ours. Definitely, salsa is Puerto Rican.

¡ . . . Salsa!

Our analysis of the characteristics of salsa has brought us face to face
with a discouraging but undeniable reality: that the Puerto Rican has not
had, at least during the present century, a rhythm—a melos—which the
world might recognize as representative of our culture. We speak of the
bomba, the *plena* and the *seis chorreao* as "our music," but look at the
battle which the performers of these genres have had to wage to survive

in the face of the unrelenting invasion of foreign tunes and foreign styles. Perhaps flowing with the current of a whole century of transculturation, the creative energy which should have gone into our own music has been ably controlled through radio and other means of communication and learning. For that reason we still lack a genre to symbolize us internationally, as the *joropo* symbolizes the Venezuelans, the *cumbia* the Colombians, the *ranchera* the Mexicans and calypso and reggae the Jamaicans. Could salsa be our musical symbol?

□   □   □

Manuel Silva Casanova, "Salsa no es nada nuevo: Curet Alonso," *Avance* (San Juan) 2, no. 57 (20 August 1973): 16-17.

Tite Curet is the composer most admired today by salsa bands, singers, and performers. Considered an authority on questions of Latin music, Curet offers his impressions of salsa, including his view that salsa music is nothing new.

Avance: What do you understand by salsa music?
Curet: Simply a mixture of bright and lively rhythms which have really always existed. Salsa as a rhythm in itself doesn't exist. It's really just a word which has been applied to this combination of rhythms.
Avance: What exactly are these rhythms?
Curet: Well, the *guaguancó*, the *guaracha*, the *son montuno*, the *rumba*, the *mambo*, the *pachanga*, with some new ideas in the arrangements.
Avance: Where did the word "salsa" come from?
Curet: Dominican radio announcers introduced the word "salsa." Later it was often heard on the Mayagüez stations, and then some orchestras began to use it, like Johnny el Bravo and others.
Avance: How do you think this new idea began to spread?
Curet: Cuban musicians definitely created the music which we now call "salsa," and it all began with the arrival in New York of some great musicians. The first generation of Puerto Rican musicians, dating from the 40s, were greatly influenced by the rhythms of Mario Bauzá, Machito and his Orchestra and Luis Varona, all Cubans. The *mambo*, which caused a real sensation throughout the United States, was introduced by Pérez Prado, another great Cuban musician.
After that, and under the influence of jazz and rock, the Cuban groups

began to vary the rhythmic and harmonic structure of their tunes. It was then that great Puerto Rican musicians like Tito Puente, Palmieri and others came onto the scene. As it was easier to record in New York, a market for Antillean rhythms came into being as a kind of musical bridge between there and Puerto Rico. And gradually, Puerto Rican musicians from New York began to flow toward the island.

The influence of the Latin rhythms developed by Puerto Rican musicians in New York has been very strong. Even the *timbal*, an instrument essential for the performance of the music now called "salsa," was introduced in Puerto Rico by Puerto Ricans from New York. Until then, the *bongó* had been used for the *baqueteo*, a rhythmical sound produced by striking the instrument's heads at the same time as the sides. Note that when Tito Puente came to Puerto Rico, Noro Morales was already famous, although he played mainly *rumbas*.

Avance: Do you see the sudden invasion of the slide trombone and its displacement of the saxophone in the new bands' arrangements as a characteristic of salsa music?

Curet: Well, the trombone was in use long before the word "salsa" was even introduced. You see, the sound of the saxophone, especially the soprano and the alto, overshadows everything else. The trombone, besides clashing less with the singer, is easier to write for. Any musician with a little skill can arrange using trombones.

As for apparent rhythmic changes in salsa pieces, there is a lot of confusion and error. Sure, a lot of sound effects and electronic additions have been introduced and the trombone has become a basic element in the arrangements, but these changes are nothing spectacular. Palmieri has used the trombone for a long time, and Mon Rivera sang his *plenas* to the accompaniment of trombones.

Still, we must accept that salsa is being described internationally as an aspect of Puerto Rican culture. But before they were known as salsa, the Afro-Cuban rhythms which form the basis of salsa music were identified as Puerto Rican. After the disappearance of Cuba from the international recording market, that whole group of Puerto Rican musicians who became prominent here and in New York since the 40s has assumed the leadership of what is known as salsa.

The Passing of a Pioneer

Edgardo Rodríguez Juliá, *El entierro de Cortijo* (Río Piedras: Ediciones Huracán, Inc., 1983), 30-39.

Yes, Ma'am, Cortijo is surely dead, and it seems like just yesterday when such a fatal fatality of fruitful life was inconceivable. . . . 1954 . . . . Cortijo wasn't only the last of the great pleneros—without forgetting Mon Rivera, of course—but he was himself the very flavor of the plena of those years of the fifties: years so distant today, years actually closer to the thirties of Canario than to our apocalyptic eighties. Figure it out: in 1954 you were twenty years away from 1934; in 1984 you'll be thirty fatal years away from those programs in which Cortijo's combo appeared in the Taberna India along with Reguerete and Floripondia. I was born in 1946, only ten years after the beginning of the Spanish Civil War. On October 9th I'll be 36 years old, and then I'll have to explain to my rocker son that Cortijo's first combo still wore *guaracheras*. . . . Guaracheras? Yes, guaracheras, those flounced balloon-sleeved shirts which the Cuban rumba bands wore: the perfect symbol of a Caribbean and Mexican tropical fantasy. In 1954, when I was a kid of eight, Cortijo's gang of blacks caused a revolution in Puerto Rican popular music by introducing the agility of the combo.

At the same time, jazz was wiping out the big band. But while jazz lost contact with the dancing which had accompanied it in the swing era, Cortijo kept the dancers, those free-wheeling exhibitionists of the *plena's* tangy *tumbao*. In this way the *plena* of Cortijo retained its deep roots in the music of the people, avoiding what happened to jazz when it became formal music, music made more for concertgoing philosophy professors than for funky dancers. All this should tell us something about the deep sense of community which our popular music still retains.

Well, then; the quartets of muted trumpets and the suffering sentimental guitar trios were soon left behind. The salon *plena* of César Concepción was beginning to sound fusty, antiquated. Rafael Muñoz was almost an arteriosclerotic myth. The Pepito Torres Orchestra seemed to be made up of starched blacks and *full-time*[41] engineers who practiced their instruments while the little woman cooked dinner. Then Cortijo arrived, with a new social presence, the force of a restless mullatodom made possible by the mobility of Muñoz Marín's industrial development program. Canario's proletarian *plena*, the *plena* of the *barrio* and the slum, now becomes the music of the urban housing project. And as if designed for this new music a new medium arises, as television becomes the stage not only for a new type of musical group but also for a threatening new social presence. The lily-white society of the grand social clubs and salons must have trembled before this new kind of orchestra, formed almost entirely by blacks. And too, the bands' dancing while they played:

how very coarse! Even worse, they didn't use printed music and their behavior on the stage was in no way appropriate for the musical formality of a proper dance orchestra. Frightful! And to top it all off, this combination of choreographic charisma and musical *showmanship*[42] was exactly what television needed.

The next Puerto Rican musical revolution would occur seventeen years later, at the other geographic pole of the social mobility of the Muñoz Marín era: I refer, of course, to New York City and salsa. . . .

But in addition to being appropriate for television, the *plena* of Cortijo was fiercely fitting for the phonograph. The crazed fans of this music identify the different phases of Cortijo's combo by the recordings which succeeded one other in dizzying sequence once those timeless tunes hit the 45s: "Déjalo que suba," "El negro bembón," "El satélite," "El chivo de la campaña," "Con la punta del pie Teresa," "Quítate del vía Perico." Quality and quantity, sonoral community, and charismatic individuality: these are the distinguishing marks of Cortijo's first combo. . . .

Women spend more time before the corpse than men do. Almost all of the men simply nod the head and go on, conscious of the terrible and solitary presence of the deceased. Women, on the other hand, stand face to face with the corpse, confronting death with the same earthly vocation which for them makes possible the savage act of giving birth. Woman is the great priestess of birth and death. For this reason if it's a question of birth you call the midwife; if it's a matter of death, call those ministering women who know all there is to know about the great moment of death: "But dearie, if she seems dead it's because she doesn't want to let go. Talk to her, pray for her, tell her that she's been a good woman, and you'll see how she becomes calmer. She hears, yes; speak to her; sure, she hears. . . ." If it's a matter of life or a matter of death, call the women. . . . The men; well, we nod our heads, we look sideways. The mortality of the flesh disturbs us. In the presence of death and illness we feel the same loathing that we experience in the presence of dirty diapers. Bred to inherit the peacock's glory, we are repelled by everything that challenges our vanity, our testicular authority. In both cases, this is simply our denial of the repugnant; more by training than by nature, we are confirmed anti-repugnant beings.

I look at Cortijo and to my surprise see the little goatee which due to haste I missed during my first curious glance. But now I'm calmer, and I can even see the carnation which has been placed beneath the tulle: one of those delicate offerings which will better safeguard the good fortune of the living than the salvation of the dead. Cortijo, like Maelo, let his

beard grow "when he was old;" he *funkeó* "to be with it in the new salsa."
All the clean shaven, from Johnny Pacheco to Eddie Palmieri, left the
papazo or the razored Tito Rodríguez-African style of the seventies and
rode the new wave of salsa-with-beard, their afros slightly greying. If you
don't believe me compare two record jackets: "Descargas at the Village
Gate–Live Tico All Stars" (Tico S LP 1155) and "Fania All Stars, Live
at the Cheetah," vols. 1 and 2 (Fania S LP 00416). On the first jacket the
performers resemble accounting professors at the Inter-American, that is,
aguacatones but respectable. On the second, the *salsa*[43] seems to have
been made with the *sofrito*[44] of black Harlem, for the performers have
begun to assume the beards, the hair and the malicious eccentricities of
the black jazz musician. The first recording is from the mid-sixties and
the second from 1971. Not a great deal of time has passed, but the
mambo-jazz of Tito Puente and Tito Rodríguez has given way to the new
sound of the trombones of Eddie Palmieri's La Perfecta orchestra: the
aggressive lumpen revelry of the *salsa guaguancó*. The Ismael Rivera of
the "Chivo de la campaña" stands aside for bearded Maelo, mandinga
patriarch of Los Cachimbos.

Then without warning or premonition appears Ismael Rivera, the great
Maelo, the *sonero mayor*, the tremendous soul brother of the *soneo* and
the *bembé*. Maelo is of average height, wiry, with those muscles of the
slum and the project which he owes as much to childhood urchinry as to
the diet imposed by *controlled substances*.[45] A little less scrawny than the
classic Puerto Rican undernourished squirt, his chest seems a little sunken
due to the tendency of the *what's happnin man*[46] housing project fuckin
lumpen Puerto Rican to hunch over. The graying beard has finally given
him the serenity of the wise old African tribal elder, a condition reminis-
cent of Charles Mingus during his last cancerous years. Don't even
mention the gray hairs in his afro, which are there as if to convince the
university girls whose musical limits are Daniel Viglietti and Atahualpa
Yupanqui of the virtues of salsa. I'm sure that if I were to show them a
photo of the Ismael Rivera of the first combo they would say "But Maelo
is much better now; before he wasn't so *nice*." What happened was that
in the middle of the seventies beards dropped their Independentist-
Socialist-Fidelist symbolism, appearing in the environment of the street
corner loafers: the subdivisions and housing projects out beyond the
Campo Rico Avenue frontier. Maybe these punks began to favor the beard
when Eddie Palmieri let his grow around 1971. Well yes, Maelo does look
good with his wise gray beard, Congo style. But this isn't the same Maelo
who sang "Quítate de la vía" and so many other hits of the fifties and

early sixties. Neither is he the singer whom Cortijo brought to the first combo from the Panamericana, covered in the glory of "Charlatán," "La vieja en camisa" and "La sazón de abuela." Then he wore his hair *permastrate* almost to the roots, a style which he would later exchange for the Tito Rodríguez razor cut. In those years Ismael Rivera had, according to the view of decent folks, one of the most wise-ass faces which Puerto Rico had produced in all of its vulgar history; that smirk and the arrogance of his glance shaped a countenance straight out of Puerto Rico Avenue, Villa Palmeras. Maelo has become serious with the years, while the beard looks good on him; with that beard he could pass for a sociologist of Caribbean literature.

Notes

1. For an account of the adaptation of Puerto Rican musicians to the working environment of New York City, see Ruth Glasser, *My Music is My Flag: Puerto Rican Musicians and Their New York Communities, 1917-1940* (Berkeley: University of California Press, 1995).

2. "El Caribe" was the *nom de plume* of the noted poet José Gualberto Padilla (1829-1896); his daughter, author of the present essay, then used the name "La Hija del Caribe." Padilla's original rhymed text is as follows: ¿Por qué nuestra descendencia,/expatriada de sus lares/tiene que cruzar los mares/siempre que busca la ciencia?

3. Núñez (1850-1915), pianist and composer, was the first Puerto Rican musician to establish an international reputation. A prize-winning graduate of the Paris Conservatory, he became a very active performer and teacher in Europe, Mexico, Cuba, and the United States, living only briefly in Puerto Rico.

4. The Ateneo Puertorriqueño was established in 1876 as a center of literary, scientific, artistic, and intellectual discourse, and remains one of the island's main cultural centers.

5. The reference is to a periodically recurring debate regarding the Puerto Rican *danza*. See Chapter 4 of the present anthology.

6. A detailed plan for organizing musical instruction in Puerto Rico, including this proposed institution, as well as the text of a resolution submitted to the Chamber of Deputies of the Puerto Rico Legislature in 1913, may be seen in Callejo (1971), 255-71.

7. A branch of the autonomous government created under Spanish rule in 1897; some of the features of this government were retained under U.S. military rule until a civil government was created by the U.S. Congress in 1900.

8. The Puerto Rico Emergency Relief Administration, a New Deal program of the United States Government.

9. Luis R. Miranda, *né* Luis Rodríguez Miranda (1875-1949), bandmaster, orchestra conductor, composer, and active participant in many other phases of the island's musical life.

10. The first generation of descendants of Jesús Figueroa and Carmen Sanabia de Figueroa, comprising eight performers extremely important to the island's msical life, mainly through performances of chamber music in different combinations and as section leaders in the various orchestras whose work culminated in the creation in 1957 of the present Puerto Rico Symphony Orchestra. See Ivonne Figueroa, "A Narrative History of the Musical Life and Contributions of the Figueroa-Sanabia Family" (Ph.D. diss., New York University, 1991).

11. Pianist Jesús María Sanromá (1902-1984) was at the time active mainly in the U.S. as pianist of the Boston Symphony Orchestra and as a traveling recitalist.

12. These orchestras, created by the island legislature in 1947, survived only until 1949. The next officially created symphony orchestra, the present Puerto Rico Symphony Orchestra, was created by legislative action in 1957.

13. The Symphonette.

14. In the author's Spanish "from Spain" usage, *música popular*, which in many contexts is most accurately translated as "folk music" or "music of the people."

15. 9 October 1986.

16. St. James the Apostle.

17. *Vejigantes* are menacing figures wearing horned masks, related to grotesque devil masks figuring in church processions in medieval Spain as well as to generalized representations of Moors. *Caballeros* represent Spanish knights. Both figures derive from the legend of St. James the Apostle appearing during the battle of Clavijo (844) to inspire the Spanish forces led by King Ramiro of León. Elements of West African religious symbols and their survivals in America have also been seen in these traditional figures.

18. One of Puerto Rico's most cherished symbols: a tiny tree frog whose call is a shrill near-octave upward leap.

19. The extraordinary cellist Pablo Casals (1876-1973) left Spain in 1938, following the fall of Barcelona to the forces of General Francisco Franco. After the Second World War he vowed never to perform in countries which recognized the Franco government.

20. Violinist Alexander Schneider (1908-1993) was mainly instrumental in persuading Casals to appear as the central figure in the Bach Festivals at Prades and was later to play a principal role in the conception and organization of the Puerto Rico Casals Festivals.

21. Casals' mother, Pilar Defilló y Amaguet de Casals, was born to Catalan immigrants in Mayagüez, Puerto Rico, in 1853.

22. Casals suffered a heart attack during the first rehearsal for the first concert and was unable to take part in this inaugural Puerto Rico Casals Festival; he returned to the stage for the second festival in 1958 and continued to

participate in successive festivals until his death in 1973. Violinist Alexander Schneider shouldered the main burden of conducting the festival orchestras while performing many other administrative and artistic tasks as well.

23. Works performed during this opening festival concert were Schubert: Symphony No. 5; Bach: Suite No. 1; and Mozart: *Piano Concerto in D Minor*, K. 466 (Rudolf Serkin, pianist).

24. The author, one of Puerto Rico's most innovative composers of the 1970s and 1980s, has taught at the Puerto Rico Conservatory of Music and at the University of Puerto Rico. A number of positive changes during recent decades in the policies of government agencies concerned with music can perhaps be traced to the untiring efforts of Aponte-Ledée and other writers.

25. Since 1985 the Puerto Rico Symphony Orchestra has been a subsidiary of the Musical Arts Corporation, a branch of the insular government; since 1981 it has been the official resident orchestra for the Puerto Rico Casals Festival itself. See Donald Thompson, "The Puerto Rico Symphony Orchestra," in *Symphony Orchestras of the United States: Selected Profiles*, Robert R. Craven, ed. (New York: Greenwood Press, 1986), 356-60.

26. Luis A. Ferré, Governor of Puerto Rico from 1968 to 1972.

27. A special Casals Festival Orchestra is no longer formed anew for each annual festival; since 1981 the Puerto Rico Symphony Orchestra has been the official resident ensemble, with visiting orchestras also presented. Since 1983 the annual festivals have occasionally programmed works by island composers including the author, in some cases commissioned by the festival management itself.

28. In 1980 the festival agency became a subsidiary of the newly created Administration for the Development of Arts and Culture, and in 1985 this responsibility was transferred to a successor agency, the Musical Arts Corporation, within which the Puerto Rico Symphony occupies a similar but separate position.

29. At the time of this interview, Schwartz was chairman of the University of Puerto Rico Music Department and a key figure in the island's avant-garde music movement. During different periods he also served as music critic in the daily *San Juan Star*.

30. These agencies later became separated, first in the AFAC (1980) and then in its successor agency, the CAM (1985).

31. In 1983 the Puerto Rico Casals Festival began to program and commission works by island composers.

32. The reference is to the Bach festivals at Prades, France, in which Casals had been the principal figure since their beginning in 1950.

33. Casals' mother, Pilar Defilló y Amaguet de Casals, was born in Puerto Rico in 1853.

34. As recently as 1949 there had been an official Puerto Rico Symphony Orchestra, a short-lived subsidiary of the insular government. See Alfredo Matilla Jimeno, "La Sinfónica y la 'Sinfonieta'" in the present anthology.

35. Rafael Hernández (1891-1965) was one of Puerto Rico's foremost composers of popular music, and one whose works attained wide international recognition. His production includes hundreds of works, some of which extend beyond the realm of popular song. His best known songs include "Preciosa," "Campanitas de cristal," "Lamento borincano," "El cumbanchero" and "Capullito de alelí."

36. Original in English.

37. Casinos are not gambling establishments but social clubs; the implication is of membership representing a particular socioeconomic class.

38. Original in English.

39. As in *jíbaro* speech. In more acceptable Spanish orthography: "¡Ay, compadre, no me hagas reir; que tengo el labio partido¡" ("Please, buddy, don't make me laugh; I have a cut lip!").

40. Centro de Re-Educación de Adictos, a social service agency dedicated to the rehabilitation of drug addicts.

41. Original in English.

42. Original in English.

43. Sauce.

44. Seasonings.

45. Original in English.

46. Original in English.

6

THE PASSING PANORAMA

Despite some performers' low regard for music criticism (except of course for favorable reviews), press commentary by informed and conscientious writers can serve important purposes in documenting the passing musical scene. Critical comment on musical events began to appear in the Puerto Rican press at the middle of the nineteenth century and has seldom been entirely absent since that time. Preserved newspaper writing on musical subjects is a prime source of historical information everywhere, and has been recognized in Puerto Rico as a valuable window to the past. The following material has been drawn from the only study which has been made to date of music criticism in Puerto Rico.

Music Criticism in Puerto Rico

Sylvia Lamoutte de Iglesias, "La crítica musical: origen y desarrollo." Investiture address, Puerto Rico Academy of Arts and Sciences, San Juan, March 1997.

The *Gaceta de Puerto Rico*, the official organ of the Spanish colonial government, was the first newspaper to be published in Puerto Rico, beginning probably in 1806. The paper remained continuously active until 1902, four years after the island came under U.S. jurisdiction following the Spanish American War, then resumed publication in 1908 and closed permanently in 1918.[1] Musical activities noted during the *Gaceta*'s early years mainly concerned the secular and religious observance of events taking place in Spain or of direct interest to the Spanish crown: royal births and coronations, the deaths of royalty or other important figures, and victory in battles. Other musical activities also received mention, and in this way we learn of the existence in Puerto Rico of

129

orchestras, bands and small instrumental ensembles.

El Investigador, first published as *El Espía*, commenced publication in 1820 but mentioned very few musical activities. On the other hand, *El Eco, Diario Noticioso de Puerto Rico*, enjoying a very short life following its introduction in 1822, was generous in musical and theatrical coverage. Following the end of Spain's second constitutional government in 1823, accompanied by the disappearance of a number of San Juan newspapers which had been founded under its liberal press laws, the restoration of the monarchy saw the *Gaceta* again dominating the field. Considerable musical activity took place in San Juan as reported in its pages and in the short-lived *El Eco*, but the publication of critical judgment regarding musical events was to wait until the 1840s.

The first manifestations of musical criticism in the Puerto Rican press appeared in *El Boletín Instructivo y Mercantil*, which was published in San Juan from May 1839 until 1918. In 1843 the paper deleted the word *Instructivo* from its title, becoming simply the *Boletín Mercantil*. The *Boletín* was rich in musical and theatrical news, and the first critical writing appeared in its pages in 1841. This took the form of voluntary comment without specific and official endorsement by the paper; contributed mainly by dilettantes, reviews were signed by such *noms de plume* as "Otro Aficionado" and "Il Dilettante," or by initials only: "M.A."

"M.A." describes a theatrical production offered in benefit of the Casa de Beneficencia, a charitable agency, in the *Boletín* of April 28, 1841, as follows:

> As for the performance, we would offer much praise and little reproach to the persons who have formed this company of amateurs. We do not offer this tribute in recognition of their having sacrificed their shyness and self-esteem in presenting themselves on stage without studies or knowledge in the theatrical art; nor do we grant them the forbearance which they request of the public in their modest announcement and in their obvious pleasure. No; ours is the unanimous and spontaneous vote of approval and justice which they deserve, without striving for it, from all who had the satisfaction of attending the theater on Sunday evening.

The reviewer adds: "Of the sung sections, it is just to say that they pleased as well; the repeated applause with which the public expressed its approval resulted not from pure generosity but from justice." He then criticizes the program's length, for he would have preferred shorter selections; however, the instrumental entr'actes were both necessary and well received.

Appearing in the same number of the newspaper was another contribution regarding the same event, this one signed "Otro Aficionado:"

> It cannot be denied that the evening was well coordinated with roles well interpreted by the officers of the post in both of the comedies presented (*Mi empleo y mi mujer* and *Gastrónomo*) as well as in the instrumental interludes offered by the able amateurs who performed them, making the entertainment even more varied and pleasant.

"Otro Aficionado" adds: "Finally, the bands of the Iberia and Catalonia Regiments very successfully performed selected pieces of the finest taste and harmony during the intermissions."

The earliest opera reviews appeared in May, 1842. Appearing was an Italian opera company; reviewed in a florid and pretentious style, very characteristic of the period, were performances of Donizetti's *Belisario* and *Gemma di Vergy*. "Un Aficionado" writes in *El Boletín Instructivo y Mercantil* of May 18, 1842:

> After so much hardship and disappointment in our theater we are finally able to attend lyric productions for which we have truly longed as a thirsty person longs for the water which can extinguish the flame that devours his entrails. May Heaven's blessing fall upon all of those who have made it possible for Puerto Rico to enjoy in its theater the sweet accents of Italian music which elevate the soul, transporting it to a region of delights, and also upon your person, Mr. Editor, whose efforts and whose devoted enthusiasm have also contributed to the attainment of our wishes.

The *Gaceta* was devoid of specifically musical subjects during this period, except for notices of the activities of the Sociedad Filarmónica. However, all of the period's newspapers offer important information in passing, such as the names of touring companies as well as those of local and visiting soloists. In addition, newspaper items inform us of an important genre of performance and social life cultivated throughout the nineteenth century: the concert-dance. For example, the *Boletín Mercantil* tells us of the 1848 festivities honoring St. John the Apostle, patron saint of San Juan. An important concert-dance took place, during which nine musical numbers preceded the dance; included were arias from Verdi's *Nabucodonosor* and Bellini's *I Capuleti ed i Montecchi* performed by Mercedes Sevilla and Julia A. Montilla.

The first newspaper to appear in the south-coast city of Ponce was *El Ponceño* (1852), which closed in 1854 and reopened in July 1855 as *El Fénix*, to circulate until 1860. *El Fénix* regularly carried a column entitled "Revista de la Capital," which described musical and theatrical events in San Juan with an occasional critical review. The paper naturally emphasized events taking place in Ponce, and provided ample coverage to such outstanding ocurrences as the Ponce visit in 1857 of pianist Louis Moreau Gottschalk and the young soprano Adelina Patti.[2]

During the following decades, musical coverage and musical reviewing increased as island newspapers were established and disappeared in cycles determined by political events taking place in Spain as well as by the island's economic fortunes. The *Boletín Mercantil* continued with musical news and reviews, as did *La Azucena*, published in Ponce for a few months in 1870-1871 and revived in San Juan in 1874. *La Lira* was published in Ponce for a few numbers in 1876, directed by composer Genaro de Aranzamendi and with such noted collaborators as Felipe Gutiérrez, Manuel G. Tavárez, and Juan Morel Campos, all composers, and writer Alejandro Tapia. The general island press continued to cover musical events, including the visit in 1875 of teenaged pianist Isaac Albéniz.

More new newspapers were launched in Puerto Rico during the decade of the 1890s than in all of the preceding period together; 103 during the first half of the decade alone. Many factors contributed to this great growth. Among these were a decrease in telegraph costs and an increase in paid advertising due to a decrease in advertising costs. Newspapers experienced a growth in circulation as papers were sold in a greater number of places. An increased liberty of journalistic expression also contributed to these developments.

Among the period's principal newspapers were Luis Muñoz Rivera's *La Democracia*, first published in Ponce and later in San Juan, and *La Correspondencia de Puerto Rico*, published in San Juan. In his *El Buscapié*, Manuel Fernández Juncos reviewed performances of a visiting opera company from Havana's Teatro Albisu, but from the standpoint of a professed dilettante.

The twentieth century saw an increasing interest in musical activities and in music criticism. The writing of professional musicians now became more prominent, in the contributions of performers and composers alike. Among these figured Arístides Chavier (1867-1942), Julio Carlos de Arteaga (1865-1923), and Manuel Martínez Plée (1861-1928).

Pianist-composer Arístides Chavier translated important texts into Spanish, including those of Robert Schumann, with whom he so identified himself that he occasionally used the Schumannesque *nom de plume* "Florestan." Chavier conscientiously kept his readers informed regarding the world's new musical trends and contributed biographical sketches of important European and Puerto Rican musicians. Among other literary activities he was a contributor to Arteaga's musical magazine *Puerto Rico Musical*. Chavier took part in a celebrated controversy regarding the merits of the Puerto Rican *danza*, a controversy which involved several other island musicians. Chavier urged the island's composers to abandon the *danza* and to undertake works of greater scope, to finally arrive at the composition of symphonic works:

> We have absolutely nothing against Puerto Rico's characteristic *danza* as long as its performance is limited to the ballroom, the only place where it can and should truly belong. Frankly, however, we cannot but offer our most energetic protest before Puerto Rico's wisest and most reflective elements—although they are in the minority—against the glorification which is afforded the local *danza* to the disadvantage of that great art which blossoms in spiritual precincts and preaches not voluptuous sensuality but the sentiments of love and human confraternity.

Manuel Martínez Plée, violinist and witty writer, responded with an article entitled "Por la danza de Puerto Rico" in which he invited Chavier to:

> Compose a *danza* yourself; you will earn the love of your country and will leave behind, like [Morel] Campos, a luminous train. Begin! Compose a *danza* entitled "The Repentant" and dedicate it to me so that my poor name might pass to posterity alongside your own.[3]

According to a recent study by Néstor Murray-Irizarry:

> Chavier believed that the critic must obey "elevated ideals" of perfection; furthermore, he must possess broad artistic culture and taste sufficiently developed to be able to duly assess the beauties or the deficiencies of works submitted for his consideration. In addition, he must possess vast knowledge of the theory of his art: harmony, counterpoint, musical com-

position, history and philosophy of music, and must have studied the most important works of the classic and modern masters.[4]

It is impossible to speak of music criticism in Puerto Rico without describing the work of Alfredo Matilla, a Spaniard who made his home here from 1946 until 1977, the year of his death. Matilla taught political science courses at the University of Puerto Rico and history of music at the Puerto Rico Conservatory of Music. He directed the Office of Social and Cultural Activities at the University of Puerto Rico and served as a consultant for the Puerto Rico Casals Festival; he was a co-founder of the Ópera de Puerto Rico company, a ranking member of the Masonic Order in Puerto Rico, and music critic for the San Juan daily *El Mundo* from 1946 to 1959. During that period he wrote more than a thousand articles documenting the island's musical and cultural panorama. A great number of his writings, edited by his son, have recently been published.[5]

In an early *El Mundo* article, Matilla observed:

> To tell the truth—the subjective truth—leads one onto terrain at once rough and slippery. But the critic is served by two convictions: one is that his truth inspires concerned attention, at least on the part of the public and of some artists; the other is that with honest and reasonably exacting criticism one contributes to the gradual definition of a general aesthetic position, although the effort be received with a certain spiritual discomfort by those who do not wish to "complicate their lives."[6]

Music criticism in Puerto Rico took a new turn with the re-introduction of English-language newspapers, absent for some years, at mid-century. Carter Harman wrote for a short time in the now defunct weekly *The Island Times*, while of much longer tenure in the island press were two other continental Americans who made Puerto Rico their permanent home: Donald Thompson and Francis Schwartz, who alternately wrote in the daily *San Juan Star* from 1957 to 1992 with few gaps. Thompson and Schwartz were not only observers of the passing musical scene, but also participants in it as instrumentalists, organizers, university teachers and administrators, a conductor (Thompson), and an avant-garde composer (Schwartz).[7]

Samuel Cherson, Cuban by birth and in exile in Puerto Rico since 1962, was a serious music lover with broad listening experience gained from his familiarity with recordings as well as from continual concert attendance and broad general culture. Cherson reviewed musical events

in the daily *El Nuevo Día* from 1975 until his death in 1993. He also
wrote about ballet, theater, art, and architecture, the last being his professional field. In Cuba Cherson had written for *Espacio, Bohemia,
Diario Nacional*, and *Combate*; in Puerto Rico he contributed to *Urbe*
and *Plástica* magazines as well as to *The Miami Herald*. It was due
specifically to Samuel Cherson that the present writer began to write in
El Nuevo Día in 1985, sharing with him the review calendar. Upon his
death she assumed the post of chief music critic.

Other musicians who served as music critics during the present
century have included Manuel Martínez Plée, Bartolomé Bover, José
María Rodríguez Arresón, Joaquín Burset, and Trinidad Padilla de Sanz,
known as "La Hija del Caribe." This noted figure, a leading writer as
well as a favored piano teacher, contributed articles and reviews to two
leading island magazines: *Puerto Rico Ilustrado* and *Alma Latina*. More
recently, music criticism has recruited a number of composers, including
the noted Héctor Campos Parsi, who wrote briefly in the *San Juan Star*.
The learned Spanish composer Ignacio Morales Nieva, his home established in Puerto Rico several decades ago, wrote in his conservative style
in *El Mundo* and shared critical duties with the present writer in *El
Nuevo Día*. Younger composers have also occasionally exercised the
critical function, including Roberto Sierra, William Ortiz and José Mon-
talvo. Finally, other musicians, both amateur and professional, as well as
lay enthusiasts, have in recent decades reviewed concerts for one or
another island daily paper. These have included such figures as Gustavo
Batista, Irma Isern, Mark Staebler, Robert Anderson, Haydée Morales,
Carlos Camuñas, David Pastor, Jorge Martínez Solá, and the noted industrialist, arts patron, gentleman pianist and then future Governor of
Puerto Rico, Luis A. Ferré.

Those acquainted with Puerto Rico's concert music scene, past and
present, will recognize from the present brief survey that music criticism
has been cultivated here by persons with a wide range of musical skills
and musical interests. These have included professional musicians,
music lovers with very limited musical knowledge, music lovers with a
great deal of listening experience and musical judgment, persons who
have heard little music, and persons with strong preconceived notions
regarding specific composers and performers. It has always been so, in
Puerto Rico as well as everywhere else in the world of music.

Music criticism in Puerto Rico has had moments of distinction when
served by persons with the proper background, knowledge, and writing
skill. Unfortunately, at the present moment music criticism is in crisis

here. Some years ago the *San Juan Star* attempted to impose intolerable editorial conditions on its corps of reviewers, resulting in the resignation of the entire staff, representing all fields of artistic coverage. At the present time only Mark Staebler remains of the *Star* music critics, with a regular Sunday supplement column dealing with general cultural matters. There is no music reviewer. More recently *El Nuevo Día* went through the same crisis, with the same result. *El Mundo*, as we know, disappeared some years ago; to our knowledge, *El Vocero* is the only island daily which publishes music reviews today.

We urge the Puerto Rican press and its managements to reflect upon the history and the importance of newspaper music criticism. This is a very significant part of the work of newspapers in the documentation of events and in providing information and orientation for the citizenry, including the active musical public and, perhaps more significantly, the great *potential* musical public.

Notes

1. The principal source of information regarding nineteenth century newspaper coverage of musical events in Puerto Rico, and one drawn upon in the preparation of the present material, is Annie F. Thompson, "Puerto Rican Newspapers and Journals of the Spanish Colonial Period as Source Materials for Musicological Research: An Analysis of Their Musical Content" (Ph.D. diss., The Florida State University, 1980).

2. See "Baile" in the present anthology.

3. *Pica-pica* (San Juan), July 8, 1911.

4. Néstor Murray-Irizarry, *Arístides Chavier: Humanista* (San Juan: Comisión Puertorriqueña para la Celebración del Quinto Centenario del Descubrimiento de Puerto Rico, 1993), 30.

5. Alfredo Matilla Jimeno, *De Música*, Alfredo Matilla Rivas, ed. (Río Piedras: University of Puerto Rico Press, 1992).

6. Matilla Jimeno, "Esencia y valor de la crítica musical," *El Mundo* (San Juan), 22 September, 1946.

7. A selection of reviews and columns by Thompson and Schwartz may be seen in their *Concert Life in Puerto Rico 1957-1992: Views and Reviews* (Río Piedras: University of Puerto Rico Press, 1998).

INDEX

ABOUT THE AUTHOR

Donald Thompson holds B.A., B.S. and M.A. degrees from the University of Missouri and Ph.D. from the University of Iowa, with additional graduate and professional studies at the University of Vienna, the Vienna Academy of Music and Dramatic Art, and the Eastman School of Music. He is a professor emeritus of the University of Puerto Rico, where he was a pioneer in the creation of the music department of that institution and served as its chairman for a number of years prior to his retirement from active service. In addition to his university commitments he has been active as an instrumentalist, conductor, researcher, writer, and editor. His numerous writings have appeared in international research journals and works of musical reference. He was co-compiler of *Music and Dance in Puerto Rico From the Age of Columbus to Modern Times: An Annotated Bibliography* (The Scarecrow Press, 1991) and co-author of *Concert Life in Puerto Rico 1957-1992: Views and Reviews* (The University of Puerto Rico Press, 1998).